Poetry 4
Our Children (Volume VI)
For Our Little Ones and Our Own Inner Child

So tiny and innocent they begin their lives as they emerge into the world and breathe their first breath, the wailing of their voices announcing their arrival and letting you know that life will never be the same. Yet, with but the closing of your own eyes, you can remember that it wasn't that long ago that it was you who was welcomed into your family, your presence forever changing your parents and the world around you.

It is with wonderment and pride that you watch your children grow and develop, their maturation as different and as similar as your own, each day filled with the hopes, happiness, sorrow, grief, and enjoyment that your parents felt. As the days fade to weeks, months to years, and the present to the future, you learn to appreciate the uniqueness of a child's personality, the person that they will become as much molded in your hands as their own.

Poetry 4 Our Children is a collection of poems designed to carry the reader along the journey of life, from birth to eternity. Each poem is like a young child waiting to greet you, each with a separate unique personality, each yearning to fill your heart and your soul with the newness of its existence.

I invite you into the delivery room. A world of discovery awaits!

Enjoy!

Robert A. Steiner
Poet Laureate

Poetry 4
Our Children
(Volume VI)

By

Robert A. Steiner

Titus Publishing
San Diego, California

Library of Congress Cataloging-in-Publication Data:
Available from the Library of Congress
ISBN: 978-1-4536052-7-1
Text design by Robert Steiner
Cover design by Robert Steiner

Manufactured in the United States of America
First Trade Paperback Edition: August 2010
10 9 8 7 6 5 4 3 2 1

Dedicated to Brittany, my best friend, lover, and muse, who has allowed me to liberate my inner child and has taught me that children are the key to our own longevity, the hope for our future, and our greatest gift.

And to the children in my life; my daughters, Tiffany, Christina, Thomas, and Vanessa, my grandchildren, Talyn, Angelina, and Jaycee, and my adopted Godchildren, John Luc and Kaylee, who have gifted me with their presence, their enthusiasm, and their wisdom.

And to all the children in the world.

Other Works by Robert A. Steiner

Poetry 4 Lovers

Poetry 4 Conflict and War

Poetry 4 Inspiration

Poetry 4 Men

Poetry 4 Women

Kate & Alexander – the awakening

Baby Bear's Shoes

CONTENTS

Tears of Joy

Oh tiny baby that kicks inside of me
How anxious you are to get on with your life
If I could read your thoughts I would surely know
That you anticipate your entrance into this exciting world
Already you know the pleasures of a gentle caress
And the closeness I feel sleeping in your father's arms
You've experienced the joys of the abundance we have been given
And tasting a simple burger and the sweetness of fresh fruits
By the kicks of your tiny feet I know the excitement you know
When you hear the barks of dogs at play
Although you cannot yet see I know that you yearn to look upon
The snow flakes as they drift just outside our windows
I can feel the rhythm move through your bodies as our stereo
Serenades you with a cornucopia of musical delights
I know you appreciate the sweet mutterings of two lovers
And all the tenderness that life has to offer
When you feel my gaze upon your dwelling
Despite all the trials and tribulations that you will one day encounter
You already know that I will always be there to watch over you
Most of all, you know the love I feel for you
When my thoughts drift to you tears well up in my eyes
And slowly fall to my cheeks
Oh tiny babies that kick inside me
Know that the tears you will soon shed
Will bring us nothing but joy

The First Step

The first step
Is the hardest
As your
Father knows

Asking one
To marry
Is how
Love grows

Your coming
Was special
Our own
True joy

Happiness created
By crying
God's gift
A boy

Our Little Boy

Your wagon sits waiting our little boy
As do your bat and pitcher's glove
We stored your dreams in chests of gold
Carefully wrapped with special gifts of love

Though still hidden you're always with us
Your little toes kick with such delight
So eagerly we anticipate your coming delivery
Praying that soon will be that special night

While we'd like to think you're a miracle
Surely God has smiled on our family from above
He made it possible for your parents to find each other
Now together as a family we're able to share our love

Sleep well our child for your day now approaches
May your thoughts be filled with such ethereal joy
Shortly you'll be free to experience the world
Adventure waits as you become our little boy

Our Best Chore

No baseballs today our little boy
Your hands too small to play the game
Hidden inside my body you don't understand
Soon you will as you grow into your father's name

Scarcely nine months ago you were a happy thought
In a short time you'll be free to run and explore
Your life will become full from what you're taught
For the world will be yours forever more

Though your space is now cramped and so tight
The world outside is bigger than you can possibly know
With two parents ready to be your guide
No greater happiness waits as we watch you grow

So hurry little man and sleep while you can
Adventure will be yours when you see first light
Your parents are eager to receive a new wonder
Our best chore tucking you in every night

Little Soul

Oh hear my voice my little soul inside
Know that a fantastic life waits out here
Dream only of a life filled with love
Great excitement grows as your birth comes near

In a few short days we'll give you a home
So different from the one you're used to
Your father and I have taken great steps
No sacrifice to costly as we prepare for you

Though my words mean nothing to you inside
Take comfort in the song of my speech
So anxious am I to hold you close by
Soon no longer will you be outside my reach

Life awaits you with such surprises and treasures
For your father and I are blessed by His hand
Gifted with our marriage and now with a son
Such happiness gained as you grow into a man

From Our Love

Such small fingers do you have
Tightly clasped around your mother's hand
Your eyes are big as you look around
It's hard to believe one day you'll be a man

Scarcely a day old yet we've known you always
Your time inside your mother passed as but a day
With a blink of an eye you went from a feeling
To the bundle of joy you bring today

Have no worries from this day forward
Your parents will keep you safe and sound
For as you grow we'll be always be with you
From our love and God's blessings we're now bound

Our Parents

I hate the fact that we all grow old
Our parents who cast us out now in need
Poor planning by the elderly never knowing
Responsibility created by our father's seed

Money is required as is our help
Punishing actions forgotten by the aging mind
Youth forgets not unpleasant happenings
Disappointments brushed aside for memories kind

Sibling bickering replace childish bonds
Currency more important than electrical pasts
Favoritism overlooked when things are needed
Blood runs deeper than relationship lasts

The desire to displace those that hinder
What happened to others returns once again
Hardships created by unfair divisions
A solution not possible until the bitter end

Remembering

I remember when things were green and blue
Where summer days were filled with fun
And we dreamed of places we would travel

I remember the little redheaded girl
Whose freckles mapped our friendship
And innocence protected the secrets that others would unravel

I remember those summer days all hot and sunny
When my mother served us frozen treats
And sweetness was served to us on a stick

I remember thinking how eagerly I wanted to get older
While feeling sorry for my aged grandmother
And cringed in embarrassment at her nervous tick

I remember what I thought were happier times
Whose days were graced with children
And laughter and giggling filled the air

I remember that friendships disappeared
When we would least expect it
And we hardly gave a thought to persons who had once been there

I remember saying goodbye to a life
While the moving van pulled away
And my mother frowned and cried

I remember the reason I must now remember
Why my thoughts were then filled with joy
And everything changed the day my childhood died

There Is a Time

There is a time in everyone's life
When wisdom has no meaning
It is a time when our heart speaks out
To ignore logic and reasoning

For such a time comes not by chance
But as the heavens have intended
A time to forget about second thoughts
A broken heart surely must be mended

When such a time does appear
You need not be afraid or have concern
This is a time to sing and rejoice
Life's lessons you'll soon learn

Mature

Though now mature I remain a young child
The desire to perform not restricted to an actor
I live my life inside a shell of aged skin
Hiding behind a façade of creams not what I prefer

The thrill of youth was given but never taken away
Inside my heart remains the thing that dreams are made of
Mirrors cannot display the excitement that still remains
Yet eyes can still blinded by those still in love

Although my feet have traveled many a mile
My joints now worn by the passing of the day
I remember when I counted my years on one hand
Memories now reserved for those that pass away

Despite it all I carry myself with the pride of a toddler
Each day still presents the excitement of a new discovery
For no greater gift could anyone have been given
His grace given for us just to live and breathe

A Day At The Beach

Supreme lightness
Fullness of being
Cool summer breeze
Calmness in the air

Children laughing
Dogs frolicking at play
Clouds shielding nothing
Motions without care

Waves crashing
Surfers go to and fro
A pelican soars effortlessly
The sand warms both soul and feet

Contentment prevails
Not a care in the world
Suntanned people smiling
What a wonderful day at the beach

For My Mom

Though once a child I am now grown
My life passing by as though a blink
From day of birth I have become a man
Becoming who I am despite what others think

While the years have taken me through it all
Success and rewards always following things gone bad
There has always been one constant in my life
One who has been there at times both happy and sad

From the start you have watched over me
An angel sent from heaven to guide my way
Though my mother you have been my friend
For such special love there are no words to say

So I thank Him each day for having you
No better mother could a man ever desire
For on this Mother's Day I say a toast to you
A mother whom someday others may aspire

The Sparrow

A sparrow did land
It's wing hurt and broken
It's life dependent on me
I looked out the window
The cold dark winter daring me
To make haste
Logic dictated that I take no action
As death was already waiting
Patiently in the tree
Yet my mind is jumbled
With heroics and caring
So I raced out the door a second not to waste
I captured the bird
And wrapped it in comfort
I placed it close to the fire
It shrieked and it cried
But I saw by it's eyes that if God permitted tears
They would soon flow
I fed it some bread and patted it's head
Seeking to assure it
That it's straights were no longer dire
Alas I fell asleep and discovered upon awakening
It's tiny soul had left
But I wish it had not been so

Heaven's Grand Design

Painful separations
Tug at my heart
I wonder about
Heaven's grand design
Fate or chance
How did this start
When I first had this thought
That you could be mine
Where were the signs
That such a smart man could miss
When I turned from reason
And saw the desire in your eyes
I now just live for yearning
I never knew love could be like this
Together forever
No longer separated by goodbyes

Musical Chairs

To go or to stay
Decisions we must make
About our future
Some chances we take

Romance and money
Seem to be key
Actions without thoughts
Sometimes we just don't see

We have it all
And just want more
Bad decisions made with remorse
The future isn't like before

We strive and we plan
Saying we do it all for you
But truth be known
We are all selfish too

Regardless of the results
No one really cares
For life is but a game
Of music-less musical chairs

A Birthday

Excitement exploded and filled the air
A birthday celebration had arrived
Balloons and presents and candles so bright
Eyes filled with sparkles and smiles not to hide

A year has passed since the last great event
It's amazing how fast they come and go
No matter how young or old we get
We yearn for a cake with candles to blow

So on this special day for you and all
When laughter and merriment fill the air
Set aside all your problems and concerns
And return to those younger days without a care

For hidden inside is our little child self
Who desires to be joyous and play
A birthday party is all that really matters
As we celebrate just you today!

To Begin

Starlit memories lay rusting in my head
Days long gone turned gray with age
Ideas once so brilliant have lost their luster
Life passes as quickly as the tuning of a page

No history written for all the masses
Nary a generation passes before we're all gone
Things held dear and protected with such devotion
Death comes too quickly for a life never too long

From the first natal cry to the whimper of leaving
The desire to achieve but a dream for most
Triumphs become foolhardy when compared to others
Greatness no longer when we become a ghost

Religion gives meaning yet no one really listens
Temples and churches but structures to wallow in sin
People journey through lives filled with sorrow
Our end comes before we know how to begin

Truth

Although I think I am so confused
Life's greatest gifts given to me so freely
Logic has given in to my internal yearnings
The decision to be deceptive made so easily

The need to conquest is but a small game
A chance discovery no small thrill
Lies encase words like chocolate covered candies
Repercussions should stop actions but they never will

I charge through life without much worry
Failures mean little to those without loss
A heart blackened by a life of indifference
The need to succeed surpasses any cost

Hope for love remains so elusive
No ideas ever formed for what it does mean
Endless nights become days of mere suffering
Salvation not possible when truth is not seen

Misbegotten Love

The startling uncertainty of life unresolved
Days grow shorter by the passing of the sun
Colors once brilliant fade so gradually
Betrayed by happiness better never to have begun

Eyes no longer able to shed a tear
Failings splashed so easily upon the ground
Things taken for granted always have new meaning
Actions once upsetting are missed when not around

Moistened lips lay perched upon romantic drought
Poetic speech falls speechless upon deaf ears
Sounds of forgiveness never to be spoken
No longer to be loved among man's greatest fears

Decisions made without thought set upon sheets
Think carefully in life eclipsed by our misdeeds
Passion begets siblings of human darkness
Misbegotten love satisfies nobody's needs

Sunset

Sunset fell upon my feet and slept
As Mother Night wrapped her veil around me
Though I could no longer see
I bathed in the beauty of the dark
My ears rejoiced in the splendor of nature's call
Heralding the hunters to gather for a feast
Small rodents scurried for burrows and safety
Knowing that nightfall was a mortal neighbor
I lit the campfire and smiled to myself
Absorbing the heat within my soul
Alone, separated from life and emotion
A living testimony to God's ability to forgive

Honor

Where does honor go
When it no longer matters
Does it take up residence
In the memories of
Shattered dreams
When did apology become
A replacement for honor
Was it so simple
To cast aside the
Substance of man with
A pitiful sorrow

The Flute

Fingers dance wildly
On a tattered piece of wood
Corralling the sounds of happiness
As they leap into the air
Smiles beam from ear to ear
Feet tap to joy accompanied by sound
Music inspired directly from the heart
The soul is soothed and bathed in hope
God's message not forgotten

Father's Day

I was never much for holidays
Until another Father's Day did pass by
My children failed to call
And I pondered the reason why

Was it because I'm not that near
And live so far away
I tried to be the best I could
Given all the things I do or say

The memories burn inside like acid
The choices we make are always hard
When they involve the lives of children
Especially when the birthday loses to the business card

I still cringe at all the special days I missed
So on this day I take a vow
To forgo all those things I strive for
I pray they'll have the time for me now

The Race

Lightness of feet
Swiftness of strength
Sinews and muscle
Extended to length

Colors flapping in the air
Warriors racing fast
Hands waving wildly
No one wanting to be last

Heads pushing forward
Voices crying aloud
The thunder of hooves
Cheers of the crowd

In seconds it is finished
The victor having won
Tomorrow starts afresh
Another chance to run

Aging

The passage of time
A bittersweet delight
The quest for maturity
Tainted by the loss of color
Minds awakened quickly
Soon slumber as fast
Memories and wonders
Fade like newspaper
The quest for success
Sidetracked by life
Final goodbyes
Pass without notice

Popularity

From forlorn days to times of grief
I trudge through life without much flare
Invisible to most I exist without hope
If I disappeared no one would ever care

No home have I or place to stay
All I own cradled in a single suitcase
The smell of fresh soap is a thing I treasure
As are coins I gather from a stranger's grace

My dreams were much like those I watch
Forgotten laughter once filled that place inside
Yet life turned upside with the loss of my job
My dignity left as did my young bride

Though humbled by misery I retain my smile
Inside my head they still laugh at my occasional joke
Despite the smell of despair I do manage to subsist
Chances so few for those now lost and broke

So I plead to you with your civil wisdom
Are there causes greater than helping those like me
Why do you not see that we also need your help
Charity seems not possible for efforts without popularity

Someday

No star will brighten your sky tonight
The heavens are filled with such sorrow
Dreams and wishes create not pots of gold
Rainbows never give birth to tomorrow

So wipe away the tears that do fall
Cry not for passions now gone astray
Let your soul seek shelter in my thoughts
The sunrise will always bring a new day

Though much older your ears hear not my counsel
Actions taken by youth listens never to the wise
Hearts will forever be broken by teenage romances
No harm in experiencing love no matter the tries

Take comfort that the road you take is already paved
Although your father and I feel your pain deep inside
For as you walk forward I'll always be next to you
Someday you'll make someone a special bride

Wondering Why

Why do the stars always appear brighter
When life is just beginning
Why do days seem so much sunnier
When bottles are just for spinning

Why do appearances mean so little
When our eyes are bigger than our bellies
Why do croissants taste so good
When filled with jams and jellies

Why do answers always follow questions
When in truth we don't want to know
Why do we dream in color
When our lives are black and white like snow

Why do we do such things
When we know it isn't right
Why can't we appreciate ourselves
When happiness is within sight

Why do we forget about love
When things turn down with sorrow
Why do we always forget
When things always get better tomorrow

On Tablets

On tablets of stone His words were given
Yet upon deaf ears did they soon fall
Burning bushes mean little to those who can't see
Graven images never answered by the gods they call

For centuries we've wandered our own private deserts
Hope and salvation possible with but a word
Instead we cast aside the compass once given
Seeking reassurance from the success we prefer

No temple carries the key to eternity
Truth lies not in men who wear holy clothes
Sacraments and water mean little to heaven
Our path to redemption only He knows

Mankind is selective in repeating His wisdom
Words often sited taken out of context
Yet we spend fortunes preparing for our passing
Forever fearful that it'll be our turn next

Poetry

I cannot truly comprehend the reason that I act this way
Nor can I really know why I say the things I say
I am but a man who stumbles with words I use to express
And I even have difficulty with the women I try to impress
But hidden in my round shaped head that loses too much hair
My thoughts are filled with visions of things that don't exist out there
So people tolerate my childish pranks and jokes I often do
Just to catch a glimpse of excitement and the poetry I write for you
For others may hate their lives or their how they spend their day
I relish my friends and the games we often play
Life is much too short to just grumble and complain
I prefer to forgo umbrellas and stand out in the rain
Poetry is but a song that plays to the audience of your heart
To make the world a better place I'll surely do my part

Christmas Spirit

I arrived today a different man
One who knew his purpose
I added a new skip to my step
The reason was because of Jesus

I've dreamed of being something else
To govern those both near and far
But in reality what I wanted most
Was to see a guiding star

I awoke quite early on Christmas morn
Bothered by things that didn't matter
Of God and Jesus I did not think
Seeking only to find pancake batter

Although my stomach grumbled aloud
And my head hurt from rum and grog
A light appeared just aside my door
And I heard the barking of my dog

Of Santa Claus were my first thoughts
Was the facade really a true tale?
I wished I had some milk and cookies
Or maybe a bottle of fine ale

But my ears did not hear bells nor deer
Or the jolly laughter of the fable
Instead my soul echoed with the cries
Of the child from the Bethlehem stable

For when I opened up my door
And gazed upon the scene before me
A star beam lit up a cradle on my porch
And showed me what Christmas was meant to be

A young woman kneeled beside a manger
Her beauty beyond what I could conceive
She stroked the head of a smiling babe and looked up
Her eyes asking that I learn to believe

A callous man I had surely been
Griping about everything that I did not possess
My mouth stood agape at the sight before me
It was only then I felt the need to confess

But before I could mouth or say a word
The woman and child vanished with the light
But my heart and soul felt alive
By the present I had been given that very night

For this I now say for all that listen
Forgo those things of riches and greed
Take care to value those persons that you love
And satisfy yourself with only what you need

Maybe someday you'll also see
The child smiling beneath the bright light
I wish you all the happiness in the world
And the ability to see life with my sight

No Summer

No summer heat do I feel today
Winter's chill is all about me
No sunshine bathes my face with warmth
White snow covers everything that I see

I yearn to enjoy the ocean's waves
As I huddle inside my down coat
I dream of the smell of suntan lotion
Exchanging slopes for skiing behind a boat

Then it is that your hand touches mine
No longer do I shiver in the cold
The emotions I feel bring such warmth
My only desire to be with you as we both grow old

My Forevers

No loss or grief do I have today
No more war do I now worry
The fear of death affects not my thoughts
I now bow away from heaven's fury

My life cut short by men much older
Wisdom forgotten with the tip of a pen
Thousands like me once ordered to fight
No concern ever over our ability to win

Kindred spirits were we when we came
Loyalty unmatched by those on earth
Onward and forward was our battle cry
Mortality precludes all reason for birth

The marching of feet once so reassuring
Marks the cadence to my resting place
No more sunsets will I be seeing
My forevers spent in His loving grace

Oh Little Children

Oh little children now take a chair
For a story I will soon now tell
Of presents and trees with lights so bright
And how Christmas was saved by a bell

Though Santa Claus has a part in this
Without him the season wouldn't be the same
This fable explains the reasons stars do shine
And how the custom of giving gifts one day came

So set aside the stories you've heard
Especially those of how Santa once came to be
Though it's true he does have reindeer and elves
The truth about Santa and Christmas you'll now see

For it was in years long since past
That Santa was a man not unlike your Dad
He went to work and took care of his children
But something was missing and he was so sad

He grew up when no one celebrated our Savior's day
No trees were decorated or presents given
Songs were not echoed to announce his birth
Nor were holiday greetings passed among men

Though Santa prayed for direction from God he heard not
No wisdom or voices did he ever hear
So he said goodbye and journeyed north by the ocean
Thinking God would listen if he could somehow get near

He followed the light of the brilliant North Star
Surely its brightness would also light his way
But after weeks of travel he was stuck in the ice
His shipmates having cast him adrift one day

Clothed in a red blanket and left with a bell
He drifted among icebergs awaiting his fate
Ringing the bell he hoped to be rescued
When all hope ended he arrived at Heaven's gate

Yet no entrance was granted and he was turned back
For our Savior appeared and pointed His way
Santa couldn't leave when he had such a duty
Who else could assist to bring faith on His day?

While embarrassed to stand in His presence
His beard white and long from his trip
Santa rubbed his belly bloated from no food
His life now filled with a cup of kindness to sip

Confusion did rain as Santa rubbed his eyes
Was he dreaming or had his prayers been answered?
Our Savior merely smiled since he understood
The journey for faith is what next transpired

He beckoned Santa to continue going North
Lighting the sky with stars so bright to guide
He asked only that on His birthday people remembered
The reason for His sacrifice to instill them with pride

So it was that Santa awakened covered in his blanket
Knowing that acceptance of the Savior took time for some
He made it his job to spread cheer and joy to all around
Bringing attention to reason that presents now come

For the gifts he now brings reminds us of that day
When the wise men came to give praise for His birth
Not matter the reason that we think we celebrate
Thanks to Santa all now know about His time on earth

Regardless of religion or what we may think
Christmas creates images of a star and a new baby
For no matter our beliefs on His day we give thanks
Prayers unified for peace on earth on some future day

Summertime

Hot summer breezes ruffle the air
Stillness becomes passion with only a stare
Long legged beauties all lined in a row
Young men with smirks just raring to go
The sun simmers both young and old
The allure of shyness gives way to bold
Summer vacation is such a sight
Especially to those with youthful delight
Who wouldn't give up the winter chill
Just to experience the summertime thrill?
So the next time you whistle that holiday fare
And huddle next to some fire out there
Remember the heat of the summertime sun
Vacations awaiting, it's time to have fun!

My Life

I watched my life drip silently away
The essence of my being spread all around
Best intentions fade so quickly when they're wrong
No chance for correction beneath the hallowed ground

Yet memories of my past I did not recollect
No brilliant light came to guide my way
My last thoughts filled with the pain of deception
Remorse not permitted for actions I now pay

Take heed you who are of the invincible age
Even Superman can feel his Achilles heel
A misspent moment drunk behind the wheel
The prospect of death ever more so plainly real

Sixteen years was all I did enjoy
My dreams still stored in places of my youth
Everything vanished in a time oh so short
That I now die my only certain truth

Melting Butter

Here I now sit in the simmering sun
No closer to water than my sink
My desk is cluttered with useless regard
How can they expect me to think

I'm paid for creating ideas galore
Of which they will sell for dollars
But without a curtain my brain just fries
Disregarded by men with white collars

Sure I get paid to do this and that
The purpose to which I'm never told
I seem to bring happiness to those that pay
Mostly people who are grey and old

Would my kindergarten teacher have guessed
That my life would be here now
She assumed that I was all washed up
Before the moon was jumped by the cow

But here I sit writing such things
That grace the inside of a card
I pen the silly little ditties
That creation of which seems so hard

So the next time you receive a greeting
On a card for practically anything
Just think of me melting like butter
Suffering for the happiness I bring

Giggles and Smiles

Laughter arose amid the chilled air
Snowballs never saved for a future day
Parents sat beneath blankets so warm
No sound better than children at play

Giggles and smiles bring tears to the eyes
Times once forgotten remembered with glee
The holiday spirit brings hope for the future
Surprises abound beneath the Christmas tree

Yuletide greetings spread life and wonder
Problems forgotten if only for a short pause
A choir of voices herald the spirit of the season
Even unbelievers take heed of the name Santa Claus

Mangers and candles and stars once so bright
Take on new meaning at this time of the year
Nothing else matters during the holiday season
Peace on earth somehow now possible here

Our Lives We Did Not Waste

Today I died while on patrol
Barely eighteen of our years
I never really knew myself
Still pink and wet behind the ears

I volunteered without regret
I joined with all my other buddies
To our nation's service we left
Protecting all from sea to shining seas

I learned as quickly as they taught
On how to kill those that do harm
Never a second thought would I make
I'd give my life before I would disarm

So it was this very day
My platoon was ambushed in the market
They told us to surrender and give up
We were just a sitting duck target

But my commander gave the sign
He just over the age for legal drinking
We cocked our weapons and fired out
Not one of us second guessing his thinking

In moments we all laid out dead
Death claimed us all with great haste
But we died doing our sacred duty
Knowing our lives we did not waste

Enchanted Lake

I sailed across the enchanted lake
The wind caressing my bare back
My sails billowed like majestic clouds
Gliding me easily from tack to tack

A sailor of not many skills
The boat appeared from almost nowhere
I could have sworn I was just sick
But now I felt free and without a care

What had happened I did not know
From reclining to sitting I did go
The sickness that had taken my life
I was cured but I didn't remember so

The skies were filled with a rich dark blue
The light was brighter than I could say
My heart was caressed and smothered in love
Never had I known such a day

From the skies such a sight did I see
Of beauty beyond my comprehension
An angel appeared before my eyes
Enchantment replacing apprehension

Not a word was spoken as we took flight
The boat sailing far into the sky
It was now that I knew where I was
And no longer would I wonder why

Flipping Burgers

I yearn to once again
Regain my splendor and riches
But flipping burgers and dogs
Is preferable to digging ditches

My walls are filled with awards
I have degrees up the ying yang
Past bosses extol my virtues
Of excellence they did once sang

My resume floats with honors
Varied experience do I possess
Success would seem assured
But my life is a complete mess

The economy took my job
Six figures is now my weight
What the bill collectors didn't take
Went to taxes for the State

Yet hope remains deep inside
A quitter I'll never be
I still smile and do my best
Success awaits for me

Each Night

I would have failed if not for her
No medal would ever adorn her chest
She urged me forward with her silent words
Counseling me to always do my very best

Her gentle touch would calm my fears
A simple smile could make the pain go away
She endured and accepted me at my worst
Reminding me to love as I passed each day

Though sometimes forgotten by my importance
No forgiveness did she ever seek to get
She judged me not though I did wrong
Yet didn't criticize me on goals I never met

No greater sacrifice could she have done
For from her being I first saw light
Although now separated by the heavens
I thank God for her each and every night

Grace

What is happiness when life is depressing
The ability to subsist limited to what we earn
Money slips between our fingers like liquid dust
Hope forgotten on luck that will never turn

God given talents lay hidden inside
Secured tightly away from those without cash
Brilliance restricted by unavailable opportunities
Potential discarded like unwanted trash

They say we are equal yet close their eyes
Salvation not visible for those who don't see
The cold touch of a needy stranger is chilling
Avoidance practiced to save one's own sanity

The desire to help is fueled by approval
Society pages adorned by those who don't care
Charity provided only if the cost is not personal
Those they pretend to help never invited there

Yet the human soul resolves to survive
Inequities forgotten when we sleep each passing day
For those downtrodden hope still does exist
His grace provided on our dying day

Fortune

Age means nothing to those quite young
When life is undefined and so unknown
Fast forward in time when hair turns gray
It is only then that we dread the chiseled head stone

For in our youth we are graced with confidence
Life's failings limited to games we play
As we mature and are counseled about abilities
Our dreams are squashed by what other people say

Worlds of wonder turn soon to sorrow
No hope possible for those with limited means
Our youth is crushed by those with good intentions
A helpful act always different than what it seems

Rainbows are given to lead us astray
Life can be wasted searching for one's gold
Too late we learn that life is about aging
The only fortune we share is growing old

Sins

Forgive my sins
As I now die
My years flying
Quickly by
A better man
I could have been
But my will
Preferred to party
A man of Christ
I should have been
A blanket
For my raiment
But I desired
Silk and lace
Preferring extravagance
Got for payment
So with my breath
The last I take
Listen to my counsel
Remember life is short
As are the days
Enjoyed only
By those still living

A Star

I see your pain but I feel it not
Your tears turn cold my heart
This time has come because of you
There was no easy way to start

You looked so great in your attire
If only your performance was the same
Instead you thought you'd mess around
Why you're here there's no one else to blame

I'm sure you thought you'd get a raise
Your peers were mesmerized by your charm
But for those of us who know what gets done
You're being here does nothing but harm

So as you leave and walk away
Know that good looks go only so far
Shaking you hips and tossing your hair
Will never make you a star

Doing As I Please

Today I finally took the time
To stop and smell the roses
I couldn't recall when I last had fun
Or took parental pride in wiping children's noses

Chaos and stress have so overwhelmed me
That I failed to take time for idle chatter
I've missed so much acquiring money and wealth
Trying to impress those that do not really matter

So today I pledge to stop in my tracks
And to allow my feet to feel the soil
For I now realize that success cannot be enjoyed
If to ourselves we are never truly loyal

I vowed right now to look into the sky
And to appreciate the feeling of the breeze
So here I'll sit and spend the rest of today
Just taking of myself and doing as I please

I Was a Father

I was a father and a dad
Three children did I have
Separated by divorce
My heart became very sad

My "ex" refused my visits
My children never knew
They thought I was missing
Forgetting about them too

I paid my court monies
To them it wasn't giving
I was just the absent one
Forgotten and not living

I tried my best to keep touch
My calls and e-mails unanswered
My "ex" declared it was my fault
To never see or have some word

So I live from day to day
Yearning for just some little notice
Hoping that maybe someday
They'll remember their nighttime kiss

Though old age now has come
My hair thinning and gray
May they always know I'll care
And still love them every day

Kindred Spirits

Oh kindred spirits buried in the ground
No faces to express your sorrow
We salute your gallantry this day
But no prayers can give you back tomorrow

You did your duty although so young
Your journey into life ended as a child
We sent you willingly to save our souls
And to protect those once defiled

How could you know what we all thought
That fate cares not about one's years
We'd done our duty before your birth
Lucky enough to survive our own dark fears

No longer will you embrace those loved
The cold grass gives no solace to those now dead
What spirit remains is kept alive in thought
And in memories stored safely in our head

Words will never properly pay our respect
To your heroism or why you once fought
Yet in your honor we thank God for you
And pray your passing was not for naught

Regardless

Regardless is just a word
That means no matter what
I'll do or say something else
Despite how deep my words cut

It is a word that just resides
In our vocabulary of meanings
We use it when we try to hide
Our lack of decision or beliefs

Scholars have amused themselves
When this word has come to pass
Its meaning is nearly lost in translation
When converted for a Latin mass

Alas it lives within our minds
A testament to our language and speech
For it exists to create the semblance of doubt
And keep truth just outside our reach

Monsters

I lost my innocence as a child
In a dark and evil room
I was the victim of a sick bastard
Who replaced my happiness with gloom

I was a bright and happy lad
Who enjoyed all that life did bring
But when the adult crushed my soul
No longer of frivolity would I sing

I was but five when fear did come
Bringing me monsters more evil than Satan
I tried my best to just forget the time
When I foolishly took that mans hand

I shut my mind to escape the pain
My body was pinned beneath his weight
I was never prepared to lose my trust
Or to learn so quickly the meaning of hate

My body was broken but not my spirit
So I blackened my memory of the attack
It wasn't until thirty years later
That I could finally remember back

Though life goes on without a doubt
And we're taught to forgive and forget
If I were to encounter the monster of my past
You can be assured he'd wish we never met

I urge you to listen to your child
Despite how crazy his words might sound
For imagination spawns from some truth
Especially when monsters are lurking around

Being Cool

My brain lies in a wasted state
Balanced precariously in my void head
The drugs have eaten my essence whole
I now waste my life in this bed

I wanted to be cool like all the gang
To enjoy the pleasures of the bar scene
We popped handfuls on our way out the door
And drank and snorted everything in between

We danced like crazy fools almost every night
Spreading excitement to all upon the dance floor
Though we remembered little more then feeling good
Then crashing like a ton a bricks upon our own front door

We had it all or so we had thought
Sex and parties were just a part of living
Then one day one of the gang just fell dead
A victim to the mindless drugs we were freely giving

Of course we thought about a quick life change
We knew our own time would surely be ending
But we had fallen too deeply into our own pit
Salvation for us would never be pending

Alas when I did one day stumble and fall
My thoughts seemingly scrambled in a pot
My twenty-one years vanished from my memory
No return policy for the drugs I should not have bought

Good Bye

Words can never truly express the things that I feel
For a sentence can never mean what I want to say
Just know that my heart is full of joy right now
For all the things you do each night and day

Though others may not see beyond your work
Or pay attention to what you do or get done
Take satisfaction in being truly amazing individuals
Who work very hard and can still have such fun

I've felt fortunate to have been accepted by you
Though sometimes even I pondered the question why
It's truly been a privilege to have known you all
I'll forever cherish my memories until the day I die

So though I'm gone and our roads now diverge
Remember that I'll always be a thought away
If you ever need anything or just need a friend
Please be sure to contact me on that day

Our Sorrow

No written word nor spoken text
Can truly express our heartfelt sorrow
Just know that you're in our thoughts
As you cope with each new tomorrow

Though we're only friends and colleagues
Realize that we consider you a relative
Take solace and see we're here for you
Gladly offering all we have to give

While we'll never understand your loss
For love exceeds what we all do know
Think of us and how much we care
No matter which road you now go

We pray you'll overcome the events of today
Knowing that each passing creates life anew
May you forever cherish the love now in your heart
Keeping the everlasting memories that belong only to you

A Pelican

A Pelican
Majestic
Sailing
High above
Gliding
Effortlessly
Upon silken clouds
Seeking only
To fulfill
God's plan
Never understanding
Why
A lesson
Learned
By all man
To live life
Without questioning
Bird and man
Both the same
Living
As best
They can

Our Cats

I stood aghast at such a sight
Our cats have had such a splendid time
They had managed to destroy the living room
But from the look on their faces it wasn't a crime

No doubt young Snickers had started it all
Giving great care to investigate the plants
Momma Kitty her apparent older assistant
Must have helped to insure their were no ants

Needless to say when the first pot fell
Tumbling from high above the floor
The racket must have been quite exciting
For they succeeded to dump even more

When quite happy with the dirty results
They duo proceeded to get food on their own
They ripped open fifty pounds of kitty food
Spreading every kibble from carpet to entryway stone

Yet not finished they found the cat nip
Gingerly dusting the house just so
When so high they fell fast asleep
No doubt thinking of their escapades we've never know

Though when I was about to scold them both
So cute they looked cuddled and fast asleep
I shrugged my shoulders and only smiled
Such a small price to pay to have to clean and sweep

Delicious Decadence

Delicious decadence covered in sprinkles
A creamy delight so sumptuous to eat
Ice cold ice cream accompanied by bananas
Excitement abounds for a summertime treat

Children's faces grinning with happiness
Anticipation for what lies just in sight
Tiny fingers tap silver spoons in rhythm
Eagerly awaiting the first chilly bite

Giggles and laughter abound with true pleasure
As bowls are attacked without hesitation
Even sharks have no chance amid such feeding frenzy
When competing with children on this occasion

Faces soon are covered in colorful goo
A supreme testimony to goodies so great
Though filled so full with such luscious eating
To start all over again they surely can't wait

Never Never Land

A simple drink was all it took
To change my world forever
I never intended I'd get drunk
And end up in the land of Never Never

How did I know Peter Pan was real
To me he was just a nursery rhyme
I should have nursed that silly drink
And saved the next one for another time

Yet I became plastered beyond compare
My brain was squishy and filled with mush
Before I knew it I was talking to a fairy
The thrill of it giving me quite a rush

Within minutes or was it hours
I found myself flying in the sky
To see the world as a human bird
In my drunken state I failed to wonder why

Then sometime later I landed somewhere
Peter Pan himself came to greet me
He welcomed me to his storybook land
And proceeded to disclose my fantasy

And so it was that I regained my youth
For no longer would I return back there
Here I remain in Never Never Land forever
To live free again without a care

I Cried Alone

I cried alone one winter night
My loss seemed beyond compare
My lover was taken before her time
Her passing was more than I could bear

Though large in stature and strong in mind
I laid crumbled in a huddled mass
The pills I'd taken were taking affect
In time my pain too would pass

Yet my lover stood before Heaven's gate
She prevented my moving ahead
Though I professed my love and asked for entry
I awoke not in Heaven but in my bed

Then it was that I understood her reason
For each person is sent on their own quest
We're required to live our lives fully
Never forgetting to love and do our best

So I cried for my friend and partner
Whose love helped me find my way
I give thanks to Heaven for her existence
And thank her for each breath of every day

A Missing Daughter

I awoke to find my daughter missing
Though she left so long ago
It's been years since I last saw her
Where she's been I do not know

I feel sorrow to realize I was remiss
To allow a child to drift away is a shame
So concerned was I with my own affairs
Regardless of the excuses I have only me to blame

A child is a living part of our being
The reason that the world does go on
They are a memorial to love everlasting
To be cherished though physically gone

I vow to do better from this day forth
To never forget the gift God gave me
Life means nothing if our children are forgotten
How important can strangers be?

Children

Brightness and beauty and all things pure
These are what children are for
They remind us of much simpler times
Before we coveted things and much more

We are the keepers of their little hearts
Yet we protect them not from our hate
Who are we to destroy hopes and dreams
When we preach about entering Heaven's gate?

They represent all the good that we were
Souls that need to be cuddled and loved
Instead we make them grow up too fast
Young flowers snapped prematurely from the bud

We are all at fault if we but think
Even those who have no children of their own
For we expose their young hearts and minds
To such things that are better left unknown

So take heed you of mature wisdom
Remember that children are our tomorrow
For if you disturb God's greatest gift
Surely your happiness will fall to their sorrow

Death

If life did end this very day
Will you care or fret?
Will you be afraid of what follows
Or have you not prepared yet?

While some may speak of brilliant lights
Or angels who guide us away
What happens to those with faults
Or those with unfinished business today?

What if hell does exist
Though no one truly knows
If you believe in God and Christ
Will you be forgiven for your sorrows?

There must be a thousand concepts
And as many religions that direct
Is any one of them really true
Or do we just desert our bodies and defect?

If death is really so grand
Why doesn't everyone just end their lives now?
Is it because we just don't know
Or that life ends sometime somehow?

I think I'm ready as best I can
If my life were to end today
Besides what can you actually do
For as with birth you have no say

The Cowboy

Alone and confused he just rode in silence
His cattle had drifted to the four winds
No longer did he have the will to give chase
And for once he regretted he had no wife or kids

He was a cowpoke by trade and knew nothing more
But for fifty years he was regarded as the king
Scores of cowboys had ridden and given their lives
And in the old days it was his tales that they would sing

Time did move on and the range disappeared
Modern technology eliminated the need for a cattle drive
He soon found less and less need for his services
With progress came changes and no more need to ride

So now he just sat on his tired old horse
A barbed wire fence barring his entrance to heaven
He simply shed a single tear as a car sped by
No more would there be a time when men were just men

My Special Angel

I've been so bitter I must say
Losing sight of what I had
Of riches and material things I lost
It seems like forever I've been sad

I was on top a mighty mountain
My name and fame were like gold
Fortune and I were intertwined
My success assured until I was old

Alas reality took a twisted turn
Everything was gone in a simple blink
What I had once was taken away
I became depressed and turned to drink

Yet a special angel was sent from above
She gave me both love and hope
Without caring who I had been
She helped me to live and cope

For it was then that I came to live
My angel came to become my wife
I am now richer that I have ever been
I thank the heavens for having her in my life

Can It Be True

Can it be true
That I'm not like you
My father lives high in the sky
Though I do live
With wisdom I give
It is now I wonder why
I've felt alone
My heart colder than stone
My life passing as blowing air
Could it be true
There is something I knew
I was sent here from there
Don't be surprised
Wipe the tears from your eyes
You've prayed for my return
Now that I do come
You'll say I'm crazier than some
And curse my soul to burn
Yet I beseech you
Forget what you knew
My father is wiser than all
For I know why
For you I do cry
I'll listen if you call

Grace

A man I once knew is now gone
His soul has passed through heaven's gate
When I first met him he was a humble man
Who eventually became someone so great

I was but a boy when I shook his hand
His smile warmed my heart and soul
What he said I don't now remember
But the feeling I got I'll forever know

For that moment in time I was so special
Though so young I felt like a man
When I walked away I was so different
Discarding sport figures to become his biggest fan

While he undoubtedly never thought of me
As he passed into his historical place
I'll forever remember that moment in time
When I stood in the presence of his grace

Youth

The smell drifted into my nose
It reminded me of life as a kid
My taste buds exploded at the thought
Of a fresh baked pie beneath a pastry lid

To be young again is what we dream
Especially when times are filled with stress
Think of being sixteen with your brain
It's truly quite exciting you must confess

To know things because of your age
No longer would you strive to study
You'd have the advantage everywhere you went
No doubt you'd be everyone's buddy

But truth be told you'd be bored
For the wonder of youth would be gone
When you remember back to your younger days
Wasn't it to be older that you did long?

Another Birthday

Once again another birthday has come
Though this time the winds of change are about to blow
The world we knew just one year ago
Will soon become something we hoped we'd never know

For on this day as you blow out your candles
No doubt wishing for happiness and prosperity
Also ask for a wish for us all
For our group will soon no longer be

Not long from now our company will be gone
Your leadership forever etched in each mind
Though history won't remember what you did for us
Know that to us you're one of a kind

So on this day we toast for tomorrows
For we'll each need to journey a new way
May God grant your wishes and watch over us all
Hoping this is your best Happy Birthday

Sensible Solutions

Sensible solutions is what they're called
Taking actions to preclude a threat
Careless decisions made forgotten too quickly
Especially if they're no repercussions yet

Simple omissions to do or to say
Made in the heat of growing romance
Hormones jumping to engage in pleasure
Forgoing discretion for just a chance

Relative time is but fleeting
From start to cumbersome end
Kisses given and taken without emotion
Black and white rules forced to bend

The death of a fetus taken without feeling
The desire to eliminate a forgivable mistake
Judgments made on what to do always
No one's choice but the mother's to make

Short lived excitement affects forever
Breath saved or taken with lacking care
Children left to make adult decisions
Tortured souls with a child to bear

Sweet Angel

Sweet angel who watches over me
I can't see but know you're there
I hear you working to assist me
Your soft touches made with such care

Though I live inside this vessel
My mind still roams with active flair
While my body remains comatose and still
If you only knew that I know you're there

Your voice gives me my only pleasure
For it calls to me in my foggy place
Had you given up on me and left
I'd have no hope in regaining God's grace

When I awaken I hope I'll recall
Everything that you've done for me
Because of your sacrifices and struggles
I'll soon return to being just me

God's Gift

The smell of salt fills the air
As the waves crash upon the shore
Hermit crabs scurry for cover
Retreating back to the ocean floor

Seagulls soar high up in the sky
Pelicans glide just above the waves
Sea lions enjoy sunning upon rocks
Youngsters search for treasure among the caves

A simple stroll along the beach
Is a pleasure shared by many
Enjoyment of one of God's greatest gifts
Cost not a single penny

Commentary

To victory! To victory!
Is all the commander said
As he unleashed his troops
Onto fields flowing red
Up the embankment
His forces did go
Into a fusillade of cannon
And the muskets below
His troops fell away
Death coming quick
The advanced mired in mud
And hedges so thick
Onward! Onward!
The commander did cry
Sending foolish young men
For their country to die
And then it was over
A new flag did arise
The enemy was defeated
Corpses covered in flies
Medals were awarded
Valor among those dead
Unheard words for those gone
Oratories left unread
As years did pass
Memories would fade
No one will remember
Those in the grave
Wars for pride
But mostly for greed
Living souls into words
Historical commentary to read

Virtues

She needed the money or so she thought
Her last job had ended without warning
For several months she had walked the streets
In desperation taking a job that lasted until morning

It wasn't so bad she had to believe
She had to pay her rent the next day
Though she would have chosen differently
Unfortunately there was just no other way

So stoic with pride she couldn't ask for help
Her parents had raised her to be on her own
She tried to make the best of it all
It is really hard to survive when all alone

Wiping a tear from her eye she did frown
Her hand taking the cash from the stand
She couldn't believe what she gave away so freely
Could now be worth five grand

A lesson learned but maybe not
A search for a career put on hold
Desperation affects the morals of us all
Sometimes turning virtues into gold

Invisible Person

I am the invisible person you don't see
I work behind the scenes and stars
I'm the one who makes sure everything works
From hotel accommodations to limousine cars

While others bask in the sure perfection
Everything made to fit just so
I'm the one who scurries around quickly
Fixing problems that they'll never know

Although others smile and take all the credit
Claiming to have managed what was done
I shrug my shoulders and get back to work
Insuring that others enjoy themselves and have fun

Despite the obscurity and being transparent
There is really no place I'd rather be
For I am the one who smiles the most at the last
When they make that big check out to me

A Birthday Wish

Today is such a special day
A birthday unlike others past
You celebrate thirty-five years on earth
Hopefully your memory of today will last

Though jewelry and trinkets are quite nice
There are other things that you seek
I'm not talking about cruises or trips
Or about material things we did once speak

For there are treasures that can be had
Although money can't buy them all
Your birthday gift comes from my heart
And not from some shopping mall

So as you blow out your candled cake
Knowing that wishes do come true
Today I give you my special gift
I want to have a child with you

Sisters and Brothers

To David, Goliath was a formidable foe
Despite how easy he was felled by a stone
To most of us the unknown is a challenge
Especially when you're facing it alone

Take heart in knowing we're all really scared
Bravery exists only when things are bad
No matter how hard we prepare for the worst
To get help and support we're always glad

Without our clothes we are all the same
Though our bodies and brains may differ
While some take pride in what they have
Others are regal in their special allure

Live each day just as you are
Take consolation in being like some others
For regardless of what we do or don't have
We are all God's sisters and brothers

Children

I wish I had more children
I know it's a surprising thing to say
Considering how much trouble they really are
And how much they disturb your day

Yet the children I had are all now gone
Their childhood nothing but a memory
I now regret not making more time for them
For I have no one to blame but me

Children are so pure and full of wonder
They create a never ending source of joy
So quizzical and full of hope
No matter whether girl or boy

Alas my new spouse would now faint
If she knew my mind had so changed
With her I'd do things so differently
Preventing the reasons I am now estranged

Sweets

I smell the sweets stored in the case
Such pastries I'd love to devour
I'm being so good on my diet
But don't get mush for an hour

I've lost ten pounds without a catch
Taking only a month to get this goal
I've been on this latest diet fad
But for some chocolate I'd give my soul

The people around me smile and eat
Succulent morsels passing through their lips
I try to restrain myself and to be good
Knowing that delights end up on my hips

Yet a simple taste is all it took
The waitress had been so very kind
I'd decided to engorge myself on sweets
Tomorrow the lost pounds I'll surely find

Our Prayers

When you close your eyes at night
At a time when you are alone out there
Just place your fingers upon your chest
Every beat a thought of how much we care

The rhythm you feel is our voices rising
Our prayers serenading the heaven's above
We beseech our Creator to speed your healing
Your recovery assured by our friendship and love

Though no words can express our feelings
Let your heart remind you of our intent
Just think of what you want to hear
And know that is exactly what we meant

For as you walk forward to tomorrow
Each day much better than the last
Take comfort that we'll always be there
For together there's nothing we can't get past

Simple

Nothing is as simple as it seems
Have you tried opening a jar of jam?
We take for granted some things are easy
Try making a dinner from Spam

We laugh at some who toil to serve
Carrying plates and passing us a dish
Did you ever try to recall what you had for lunch
Try remembering for a hundred others for a switch

As you proceed from this day on
Give more credence to the trivial task
For some day you'll need some help
And may be embarrassed for help to ask

We Are Gathered

We are gathered on this special day
To celebrate the matrimony of you two
Of great joy and happiness do we pray
May all your dreams and wishes come true

We've known you both for what seems ages
Though time has no meaning since we've met
You've both changed our lives for the better
No doubt that the best is to come yet

So as your hands do touch and meet
Rings exchanged as vows are said
Know that we'll always be there for you
So remember us when these words are read

For from this day forward as you do go
A special couple blessed from the heavens above
No matter where life does take you
Know you'll always have our friendship and love

My Place

So soft and silky to the touch
It keeps them coming back for more
More comfortable than almost any place
A trusted confidante behind my front door

Though rarely seen except by some
It is a place where dreams do come true
It has seen me at my best and worst
And engaged in things others wished they knew

Of all the places I have ever been
No other location means the same to me
For when I am home and all alone
There is no other place I'd rather be

That I adore my bed I do admit
For I share it with those I care
It would be much more special for me
If I found a husband to join me there

A Better Day

Does pretty mean anything if you have no sight?
What definition could it possibly mean?
If you cannot look to decide for yourself
How could you judge what you haven't seen?

If your ears never heard truly great music
Would you understand a much better sound?
Could you really discern what was really good
Or would you take the opinions of those you hang around?

We are such lucky creatures of nature
Most of us blessed with many senses for living
Yet we base our decisions on what others say
Preferring to read, watch, or listen for the opinions we're given

Take heed to live life just for yourself
For you have the ability to decide all alone
Don't let others control or rule your life
Your opinions never need to be cast in stone

So set aside your favorite magazine or TV show
And refuse to believe what they are trying to say
Look upon all you meet with a wide smile
For if you do you'll always have a much better day

Longing

Poetic words from the fool's folly
Comedy misplaced by romantic pain
Tears fall not from laughter
Reminders to a lovers refrain

Hopeless attempts to regain composure
A moment lost to hurtful prose
Salvation not made through thoughtless actions
Yet a smile awakened by a single rose

Turbulent times bereft of emotion
The clock ticks away the age of reason
Souls pass alone in the night
Leftover victims to a lover's treason

Forgiveness requested in pleading words
No victory ever made in love or war
The need to be held and loved as a person
Should leave no one longing for more

Nature's Beauty

Nature's beauty taken to flight
Creating such a wonderful sight
Bright colors all aglow
Spreading wonder wherever they go
Wings flapping quickly without a sound
Poetry in motion as they move around
Spreading creation from here to there
Days spent freely without a care
Lives cut short but work soon done
Miracles abound with the falling of the sun
Others do follow as day replaces night
Nature's beauty taken to flight

Rekindle

Why can't I feel my heart beating
When you approach or go far away
Once you were all that I thought of
No matter the occasion or time of day

You are the reason that I do breathe
My love for you will never change
What has happened that the excitement left me
I feel so all alone and very strange

Is this what happens when we get what we want
No longer needing to strive or fight
If it is I'd prefer to be a failure
Just to regain what we had that first night

Though not brilliant I do understand
They say that acknowledgement is a start
Know that I'll spend my days striving
To rekindle the fire in my heart

Little Child

Oh little child who lies inside
Can you feel our excitement brewing
Do you dream about what you hear
Or about things you'll soon be doing
Are your senses alive and awakened
Especially when we embrace your home
Do you understand love and caring
Even though you sleep alone
Have no fears our little angel
A world of wonder awaits your birth
Know that your parents adore you already
Eagerly awaiting your arrival on this earth

Life

Somehow I never knew about life
Although I should have expected it at birth
I had been an all knowing soul
Whose time had been detailed to earth

While I've been called many a name
My mantle was ordained with idols and prayer
I wasn't prepared for what I assumed
Was to be a mundane existence down there

As a mighty being I was the master
There wasn't anything I didn't know or lack
Yet upon my birth my wisdom was scrubbed
For once born I could not go back

It had been a challenge of the noblest kind
My companions dared me to be among them all
But when I appeared I couldn't care for myself
And lacked the knowledge for their help to call

They must have been very amused
As I spent my years working to make my way
It wasn't until I nearly lost my mortal life
That they forced my to ask to live another day

For in a brief moment I knew all about me
Yet I yearned to remain just as I was
A simple human just happy to be
Doing things without purpose just because

To see life through a mortal's eyes
Is to understand the true gift of life
Oh how lucky people are just to exist
Through all the happiness and strife

Fabled Friend

I toast to you my fabled friend
Whose wisdom exceeds that of mine
You bring joy and happiness to all
Without a doubt you are one of a kind

You help old ladies across the street
Insuring they are well before you leave
You volunteer your time to charities
And bravely wear your heart on your sleeve

You're always there no matter what
It seems like problems are never inconvenient
You'd give your last dollars to help
And think of good no matter what was meant

Alas I now bid you adieu
As we part and go our separate ways
I'll always treasure the time we spent
Forever grateful that we shared such days

What Is Love?

What is love?
Really
Two hearts
Beating
As one?
Sometimes
Separation begets
Longing
Hopefully
The thought
Of losing you
Unacceptable
Why do we
Forget
So quickly
Longing
To Remember

Broken Heart

I felt the pain so deep inside
My heart was near to bursting
I'd searched so long to find her
For her affection I'd been thirsting

So close by yet so far away she was
A phantom to those who do see
If only I had done something different
She might have stayed with me

My words had wounded her fragile soul
I'd taken pleasure in stabbing deep
To have the ability to take back what I said
Would have given me pause to sleep

Yet love does have a weakened shell
Never meant to protect us from pain
For it bares us for others to see
Protecting us not from actions we should restrain

No matter how great or smart we are
We sometimes fail to appreciate what we found
To often we give in to greed and avarice
A broken heart never makes a sound

Darkened Wisdom

Darkened wisdom beset by dreams
Held hostage by thoughts of wealth
Logic misplaced by frivolous actions
Being true to no one but yourself

The gold coin misplaced by greed
Costs far more than it is worth
Precious gems and minerals remain hiding
Elusive wealth for those on earth

Value placed on things without virtue
The honor of one's word a silent lie
Roads taken without thought or remorse
Lend no substance to those that die

Take heed in who or what you are
Life passes quicker than the falling sun
Remember that some things aren't meant to be
Waste not your life before it has begun

Friends

What is life without friends?
Is it the sound of emptiness
You hear when you awaken?
Could it be the darkness
From which light comes naught?
Existence among solitary souls
Results in wasted flesh and blood
Awaken oh foolish one
Shyness is not becoming among the lonely
Serving to benefit no one
Let the smile overtake your face
And extend your hand to others
What is life without friends?

The Logic of Youth

How can you dispute the logic of youth
When they carry out our given orders?
We train them to lie, cheat, and steal
And to think nothing of crossing ethical borders

From TV to movies we educate them so
We teach them about success and greed
Rewards are given for deception and mistrust
Reinforced by magazines and books they read

The American pie can no longer be eaten
For virtue now rots away on the tree
Sportsmanship and honor are given no meaning
What we have wrought is now plain to see

His Glory

Why do preachers sometimes claim
They hear the voice of God
When their own sorted lives
Would make His son sit and sob?

If they truly hear His voice
Don't you think we can too?
Do you think God really needs agents
If he wants to speak to me and you?

What is good or even bad
Seems to differ among His peoples
For we commit war and atrocities
Seeking forgiveness beneath church steeples

You needn't sit within a structure
To know what He is truly saying
Merely read His book page by page
Salvation cannot be gained by paying

So take some pride in your own life
No matter how great or ordinary
For we are all important to Him
All souls made to serve His glory

The Cradle

My hand rocked the cradle
Pushing ever so softly
The baby was safe inside

It was such a miracle
That a child was here
A precious gift from my bride

Though several years older
I'd almost forgotten
What a family can truly do

Had I listened to my mind
I wouldn't have known the pleasure
Of such happiness with you

So here I sit
Just spending some time
Rocking her gently to sleep

Knowing such joy
With you and her
Makes my heart now leap

Thin

The sunshine beat upon my head
My perspiration flowed in a river
I was running to get fit
And to detox my kidney's and liver

The path was both up and down
My legs were pained and hurt
I took trails both near and far
Over hot pavement, grass, and dirt

Though not new to this running sport
My joints were made to swim
But since the diets didn't work
I decided this was my way to get slim

Although I knew I had gone far
The distance had grown so fast
Now I had to figure a way home
For the return trip I wouldn't last

But I gave it my all for this task
For surely I had to now win
So I did manage to get back home
Nearly killing myself to get thin

Celebrate

Today I celebrate this final tale
For it marks a turning point
It represents how I've struggled
And deserve a vodka at some liquor joint

It is these words that sing to me
They mean that I am now done
No more do I need dream of poetry
Its time to have some needed fun

So as you read this little tale
Know that everything has to begin
Work hard and set goals for yourself
And in the end you'll surely win

Believe

Who could have believed the things we heard
About how they treated prisoners and women
Would we have known what they had done
If a captive hadn't escaped from the prison

While some things do happen in fields of war
And the days that follow killing and dying
But to see we are no better then them
There is no more room for excuses or lying

We are the proud of a civilized state
Who have waved our flag with great fanfare
Now we find out that our soldiers are thugs
Is it any wonder the world hates us out there

The stars and stripes mean so much to us
Those who work hard to do our best
But to find out that evil resides among us
Brings nothing but shame and humility to the rest

While we have little power to put an end to this matter
Take heart to know we can change those who lead
For if retribution is not dealt harshly to the guilty
We can elect honest men versus those who prefer greed

Lonely

They say I'm lonely but I'm not
Though I can count friends on one hand
I love my life and who I am
And am confident in being a solitary man

I have scores of people that I see
Although business is the main reason
We're friendly enough and go out often
But mostly these times aren't fun

I live my life mostly in my head
My words breathe life to my soul
I achieve the greatest of thrills
When onto a page my thoughts go

So take counsel those who fret
And worry that my friends are few
Never am I let down by my thoughts
Or have never not liked a word I knew

The Wish

I dropped a penny into a well
And watched it hit my mark
I was just about to make a wish
When the sky became gray and dark

A voice bellowed from deep below
And cautioned me to choose most wise
Needless to say I nearly peed my pants
Not knowing the origin of these cries

I regained my composure and looked around
I spoke as best I could
I asked who was addressing me
And answer to get I hoped I would

A moment later the voice did speak
It told me that life wasn't what it seemed
It counseled me that I could wish for peace
Or for all the wealth I had ever dreamed

My mind was filled with visions of cures
The hurt and sick arose from their beds
Weapons of mass destruction were destroyed
And helmets flew skyward from warrior heads

And then I saw the look of wealth
Women and splendor were at my feet
I had more cash than everyone
And my picture adorned every city street

To choose between the two was quite hard
For I had suffered through bankruptcy and pain
I knew both sides of the coin I had tossed
And either decision held much for me to gain

But I delayed for a moment just too long
For another coin broke the watery surface below
I turned to see who had done such a thing
My wish was gone but I prayed it wasn't so

I yelled for the voice to return and speak
But it was the stranger who now talked to me
He said I seemed in such a horrible mess
That he wished for a moment of peace to come to me

Without another word he turned and left
And no matter how many coins I did throw
The voice never returned to speak to me
Of my choice the world would never know

Commitment

What makes some like the same
The other persuasion never does a thing
They are so enamored with just their own
That they'll forgo ceremony and the marriage ring

Though called crude and nasty names
They continue to stay their course
They submit themselves to vile and evil words
But refrain from attacking the cowardly source

Though others snicker when they walk past
And chide them for the love they bear
They'd sooner let the insults drift away
For such unkind words they do not care

While their love is hard to understand
It seems unnatural to those who don't
They are committed for their loves
To change they know they never won't

Girls

I once was just a little boy
No knowledge of love did I know
Girls were just different somehow
Neither buddy, friend, nor foe

Then my voice changed one day
My face became rough with hair
My arms and legs sprouted like beans
And other things did change down there

It was then that my temperament changed
Girls were something I came to like
Unfortunately I was young for driving a car
And dates didn't quite work on a bike

From first blush to kiss happened so fast
My high school days past with crushes
It was during those formative years
That I learned about sororities and rushes

Yet it wasn't until I saw your face
That I knew what God had intended
For when I took you for my wife
My search for happiness had ended

Dancing

Flamenco dancers on the floor
Dresses twirling up high
Heels tapping upon the ground
Performers seeming to fly
Excitement fills the air
Music reaches a crescendo
Beating hearts joined as one
Lovers sliding toe to toe
Smiling faces grin with glee
Emotions are filled with passion
Entertainment provided at little cost
Dancing brings such satisfaction

Lost Inside

Somehow I seemed lost inside
My mental capacity was diminished
I couldn't collect or remember thoughts
Counting each second I wished the day was finished

My brain was but a grayish mush
No longer did my intelligence mean a thing
I was but a simpleton in love
Thinking only of romantic sonnets to sing

How could such a man as I
Who held himself in such high stature
Succumb to the frailties of the heart
And give in to the seductress' allure

Had I not caught a glimpse of this goddess
Or let my nostrils inhale her devilish scent
I could have prevented such a thing from happening
And into a different direction I would have went

But here I now sit in a huddled mass
My heart bursting forth in joy
Just throw a beautiful woman into our lives
And even the strongest man will turn into a boy

The Leaf

A fallen leaf upon the ground
Discarded by its mother
No longer having any use
Pushed aside for another

A simple life as it was
Spawned in early spring
Bursting forth in happiness
Shading birds as they did sing

From cool nights and mornings
To scorching hot summer days
It spent its life on a limb
Pleasing to a passing gaze

Yet its time was quite short
Dispatched by a winter breeze
It joined its siblings in the air
Scattered amongst the trees

Though left to pass all alone
Its existence fading quickly
It spent its life as a leaf
To be enjoyed by you and me

Our Toast

We raise our glasses to just you two
And toast for much happiness and joy
Who would have guessed that an arranged date
Would eventually bring a lifetime to enjoy

While fate or chance or maybe the stars
May have insured that your paths met
To know that fairy tales do come true
Will surely convert skeptics to romantics yet

So as you embark to your marriage vows
Becoming as one as you face tomorrow
Know that your friends pledge our love and support
And will be there throughout times of good and sorrow

Remember forever the magic life has given
Despite the successes and challenges you'll meet
Know that you've been blessed with each other
Once just two wandering strangers on a street

Brothers

As we had planned the end came slow
No death drums for the weary
No trumpets or guns sounded a salute
Even the day turned cold and dreary

Without fanfare we were given the news
Our leaders read from scripted text
Their words heralded the worst of news
For on the list of farewells our time was next

We've known our end was well at hand
They had told us our days were numbered
But we had prayed for help and salvation
And for months we just rested and slumbered

So on this day that will be our last
We say goodbye to friends and others
We leave only with our experience and memories
Forever will we remain sisters and brothers

The Fairy Tale

A dog, a turkey, and a cat
Walked across the fairy tale land
From mountains to green countryside
They traveled upon parchment and sand

A ragged group of creatures they were
No fable or story to guide their way
They were just some passers by
Forgotten characters without a story or play

They searched for work but found not
For modern children had their TV
None really cared about old tales
When the Internet could provide what to see

And so it was that they nearly departed
Almost erased because young minds didn't care
They found a new life on the page of a poem
And in the minds of other poets out there

Now they live in the minds of young and old
Those that take pride in what they read
For from the pages of poetry imagination grows
Providing an escape that everyone needs

Your Man

Oh ye women who've lost faith
No man to warm your heart
Why do you give up so easily
When your species is the one so smart?

You are not affected by our two brains
Nor do you have our wondering eyes
You control the destiny of all humanity
Within the warmth of your inner thighs

Regardless of your shape or size
Your nationality or language doesn't matter
While we may profess a preference for breasts or hair
You control us with senseless idle chatter

We are men who love all girls
Our search is also an endless thing
You need only engage in conversation with us
To have us thinking of engaging in a fling

So forget about your hunt for love
Or finding the man you think is right
Just steal the pages from our game plan
And let your hair down just for one night

For despite how we act or do talk
Or tell you how grandiose our big plans
You just need to pay us a little attention
And post haste you'll have your man

The Bath

The jagged glass cut across my wrist
No pain did I feel or avoid
I had given up on my life
My departed lover had left me destroyed

I had lived just for the two of us
I gave until I had no more
Regardless of the cost or expense
Never did I think of trying as a chore

She was my dream of perfection
It was what I had been waiting
I gave her everything I was
Never did I believe she I would be hating

My friends tried to raise my spirits
They forced me to see other women
Despite their best attempts to save me
To put on a happy face I could not pretend

So it was that I sat and wrote a note
And thanked all who had seen my sorrow
I told them that I didn't want to lie
For to me there would be no tomorrow

Alas the blood does pool and grow
As I sit in a bath now turning red
My eyes grow heavy as I do now smile
No alarm clock to awaken me from this bed

His Child

What if you were suddenly awakened one day
And realized you were His child?
Would you change your life so quickly
And seek to bring justice to those defiled?

Would you alter how you went about life?
Would you change how you viewed things?
Could you forgo your material pleasures
Or such other items that money brings?

How would you see the injustice in life
Or deal with murder and our wars?
Would churches offer you hope and comfort
Or would you preach outside their doors?

How would you deal with religious beliefs
Especially those that deny your existence?
Would you seek to bring peace to all
And bring harmony to religious resistance?

Would you be willing to die on the cross
And give your life so others would live?
Could you learn to love everyone so much
That for us your blood you would give?

But just think for a moment or two
For in reality you are His child at birth
Will you now awaken from your slumber
And help bring peace to all men on earth?

Summer Rain

Boredom floated across the room
A summer tainted by falling rain
Board games scattered across the floor
Painful reminders to monotony
Frivolity caged within cedar walls
Yearned to escape the wooden prison
Fertile young minds preparing to explode
Restrained only by adolescent conformity
Alas a leader does emerge
Promoting screams of disobedience
A flurry of movement exits the door
Preceded by balls and gloves flying
Though wet and soaked within minutes
The shrill of joy and laughter abound
Childhood memories take root and grow
A summer camp to be remembered

Sleepless Nights

Who could dispute the facts
Pregnancy gotten by misbegotten deeds
Innocent flirtations turning to sex
Forgotten lectures about birds and bees

Where was restraint amid rabid hormones
Common sense succumbing to the drink
One's future lost in the elixir of music
Consequences distorted by the failure to think

Too young or too old doesn't matter
When frivolity gives way to delights
What had been just minutes of pleasure
Will soon turn to sleepless nights

War

Gallant soldiers all covered in dirt
Marching on the road to war
Never knowing where they would go
Through wind, rain, and snow
From battle to battle they did walk
Medals dangling across slumping chests
Victories mean little to those gone
A dead soldier forever rests
Regardless of country or flag that flies
Men rally to take arms to kill
Most never really know why there is no peace
Perhaps they never will

Nature's Beauty

Nature's beauty taken to flight
Creating such a wonderful sight
Bright colors all aglow
Spreading wonder wherever they go
Wings flapping quickly without a sound
Poetry in motion as they move around
Spreading creation from here to there
Days spent freely without a care
Lives cut short but work soon done
Miracles abound with the falling of the sun
Others do follow as day replaces night
Nature's beauty taken to flight

Chivalry

What ever happened to chivalrous men
The ones who opened doors and stood?
Haven't we taken equal rights too far
When gentlemen no longer act as they should?

Simple courtesies seem a thing of the past
As men ignore women, sad but true
Good manners I guess are no longer learned
For their usage seems the exception to the rule

Did the quest for equality kill an era
A time when men tilted hats and did smile?
No longer do you find a woman's hand lifted
Or for a man to ask permission to sit for a while

Bar stools have replaced the couch
A father's permission is no longer required
Men and women just cavort in the open
No pageantry for children soon sired

I would attest that life does go on
Past habits and practices cast astray
But don't you ever think what life could be
If we returned to days of chivalry one day?

Peace

A dove flew up into the sky
A beauty to behold and see
An olive leaf dangled in its beak
Bringing peace for you and me

How could something so simple be true
That a bird could end a war
Is it any more ridiculous it seems
To permit man to kill as before

Why do we strive to have what we want
When the price is paid with dying
Even if heaven is our final home
Is it worth the suffering and crying

Take heed those that want more
For God's vengeance is at our gates
He's blessed us with our lives of our own
For retribution comes to He who waits

Running

The pounding of soles
Upon the ground
Feet moving fast
Legs pushing forward
Stretching their muscles
The finish comes at last
The race goes on
The runners do tire
The end comes in sight
Competition approaches
The sprinters duel
Fatigue succumbs to might
Only the winner
Crosses the line
Victory taken in stride
Consolation follows
Even losers rejoice
Triumph in personal pride

Friends

As we make this final toast
We shed a tear for joy
Chance did surely let us meet
Of good times we did enjoy

But as with years things do finish
For this journey is about to end
The winds of change have come again
Into a new direction our lives we do send

We've seen the laughter and the tears
And watched our lives change and grow
Yet we've always known someone cared
No matter how bad or good things did go

Of families we will always love
For they are the river of our existence
But friends are the ones we rely upon
To help us overcome issues with persistence

So as we close this special day
Our plates and glasses nearly empty
Let us remember what friendship means
And how good life can truly be

As we journey our separate ways
Maybe never to see or meet again
We give thanks for all God has given
And how great being friends has been

Life

A silly disease did claim my life
I knew but paid no heed
Drinking and unprotected frivolity got me
Creation bringing death through my seed

I should have known as I did
But youth listens not to reason
I thought I was the invincible being
Now lucky if I see another season

I lay today in the bed I made
No longer enjoying the pleasure I had
I live just to survive one more day
Foolish intentions turned bad

God's Gift

The smell of salt fills the air
As the waves crash upon the shore
Hermit crabs scurry for cover
Retreating back to the ocean floor
Seagulls soar high up in the sky
Pelicans glide just above the waves
Sea lions enjoy sunning upon rocks
Youngsters search for treasure among the caves
A simple stroll along the beach
Is a pleasure shared by many
Enjoyment of one of God's greatest gifts
Cost not a single penny

Doubting Thomas

Doubting Thomas is what he was called
For he never trusted what others said
He forever complained of how others did things
As nothing could penetrate his thick fat head

He complained and moaned about everything
No matter how good or excellent it was
He turned waitresses into babbling masses
And made salespeople begin to cuss

He didn't care what they said about him
He disregarded anything that burned his ears
He preferred to denigrate everyone around him
And gained satisfaction by turning smiles to tears

But poor Thomas should have known things change
Because when one day as he choked on an apple seed
Those around him doubted he could be dying
To late to learn being believed was a basic human need

The Poet

I love to write as it comforts my soul
I enjoy the feeling of words that flow
Like a river of thoughts they cascade on paper
That spill forth both to and fro

Though many a passage are barely alive
Others spring forth life from the heart
If my characters mean something for just one
It embodies my courage to again start

So I harvest the delights that role from my tongue
And plant ideas and thoughts from which others grow
Though a pauper compared to others out there
Happily I'll write for those and I do and don't know

Them

I stood still in the darkened room
And felt the presence of others
There is no way to explain my emotions
For I was in the company of my brothers

I saw them clearly in my mind's eye
Their goodness painted in a moving light
I knew then that science had no answers
For things that go bump in the night

Of ghosts or angels I care not what
I just know what I believe
They or she or it had come
No greater gift could I receive

I cannot explain what God has intended
Nor if the Church knows what to do
Call me crazy but their existence is real
I only wish you could see them too

Unlike some I fear not for my death
For I know that something truly does follow
Maybe one day I'll know why they're here
But if I'm lucky I'll just see them tomorrow

My Life Long Love

My heart lies broken
Shattered to my soul
My life long love is gone
Though angels came
And took her home
I feel so all alone
If I could cry
Rivers would overflow
Sorrow swept out to sea
But my eyes remain dry
For happy thoughts abound
My memories comfort me
Just one last kiss
Is all I request
To say goodbye
Just one last time
I'd sleep my final rest
For my love
There can be no other
My heart I gave to thee
Soon I'll come to you
My life long love
Together again we'll be

My Friends

I gave my friends up for a girl
For intimacy they couldn't really give
I immersed myself into her world
Forgoing the way I did once live

Aside from calls from this young girl
My phone remained silent and cold
No more did I get invited to go out
No longer would there be stories to be told

For the first few months I had it all
My heart was filled with hope and joys
Then I began to miss my drinking pals
And I yearned to be one of the boys

Although I should consider myself a lucky man
A beautiful woman now stood by my side
Without friends how can there be happiness
Would things be different if she were my bride?

So I decided without much fanfare
That I was too young to settle down
I said goodbye to that lovely girl
And called the boys to celebrate downtown

Now my phone rings all night long
My friends call whenever they are able
Though sex and love are now hit and miss
I always have friends gathered around my table

Pets

Did you ever wonder what your pet sees?
Or ever what they are thinking?
Did you ever think that if they could talk
You would soon contemplate heavy drinking?

We pet them so and avoid them too
Ignoring them except when we want attention
What if our roles were soon changed?
Would they do the same without hesitation?

We call them our buddies and special friends
And mostly we see to their needs
But how often do we just turn away
If only to accomplish other deeds?

Since we were all created from above
All children to our knowing Creator
Don't you think there's a reason pets exist
Giving some time to think now and not later?

Though pet's forgive and love us most
Despite what the rest of the world knows
Take time to enjoy and value such friends
For they are all God's living souls

A Special Place

Oh darkened clouds up in the sky
Stay overhead and do not fly
We seek your riches upon our heads
Gentle rain to soak our crop's beds
Drought has taken many a child
Our cattle freed to just run wild
Crops have died and faded away
Grass once green is mottled and gray
We subsist on His grace alone
Those who didn't rest beneath cold stone
We seek no miracles beyond our hope
Our water pails dangling empty by rope
And then the skies thunder a murderous sound
As small raindrops soon splatter the ground
We soon give thanks to His almighty grace
Disaster averted for our special place

The Kindergarten Zoo

A dog, a cat, a parrot or two
These are things that go to school
On special days made to share
From tiny children without a care
They laugh and they grin with a devilish smile
Being good and sitting still for a while
They enjoy life and all its pleasures
Eagerly sharing their sacred treasures
So Rover and Blinky and Kitty too
Become visiting members of the kindergarten zoo
As parents come with cameras a glare
Clicking pictures madly of their child over there
But things will end with the blink of an eye
And memories of kindergarten will fade as the years go by
So remember the lesson you learned while still there
That life brings happiness when you bring things to share

Tranquility

Cool ocean breezes
Play upon the skin
Palm trees sway
In the calming wind
A lazy summer afternoon
Sunbathers in a row
Relaxation abounds
From head to toe
Vacation has come
For the lucky few
A time for recovery
A soul to renew

Women

I seem to fall in love
Almost each and every day
Its because I adore women
Regardless of what they do or say

Their curves and hair make me smile
I enjoy the things they buy and wear
No matter their size or even their color
I find it impossible not to stare

Since I travel throughout the land
I can't avoid the female form
All lands should take pride in their women
For beauty there is no such thing as the norm

So you who are of the fairer sex
Who rule the hearts of mortal men
Please don't worry what the media says
Why would you want to change God's perfection?

Fame

No one really cares what I say or do
When I have money or a famous name
I am the envy of every working person
A world of copycats hoping to be the same

I can have sex and tape the affair
My indiscretions spread across the Net
But the media adores my virtuous image
Preferring to show pictures of me with my pet

Politicians and leaders bide for my time
A photo shoot with me is what they seek
They say not a word when I'm screwing their daughters
For the sake of reelection they turn their other cheek

The fans all adore me and what I wear
Regardless how I try to dress poorly on purpose
Fashion designers go crazy to do the same
Not realizing that they should just never fuss

But then it will end as all things do
My image will be a thing of the past
No one will really care what I say or do
So I might as enjoy things while they last

Weight

I saw an ad in some magazine
Selling what who knows or cares
What I really noticed was those abs
No doubt the epitome of envious stares

I patted my belly and made a frown
My spare tires sagging around my gut
No Atkins or South Beach could now help
When I yearned for a Krispy Kreme doughnut

I've tried and been good many a time
Giving my life to the devotion of exercise
But having fasted and worked off the pounds
I did nothing but regained weight and my size

So here I now sit in a chair
My bottom wedged so deeply in place
Why should I worry about my weight
When I would weigh nothing in space?

Love Endures

A simple smile
Across
A face
Signaling hope
Along
The way
Two hearts
Separated
By fate
Coming together
A simple kiss
Given
On lips
Love endures

Fat

A simple molecule of some fat
Spawned some days after I was born
Traveled around my inner self
Feeling lonely and forlorn

Then one day he had a thought
Of playmates did he envision
He wished to never be alone again
To this end he started on a mission

He spent some time at the brain
Who regarded him with confusion
For although Fat was supposed to be bad
Obviously the eyes were blinded by illusion

The taste buds agreed and did concur
That Fat wasn't such a bad guy
For when they met Fat's other friends
They invited them in to sit and lie

When the rest of the body heard
That excitement came in all tastes and flavors
They invited Fat and his friends to visit them
Forgoing keeping fit and other such silly labors

So the years did pass with major girth
Fat taking my body for his domain
Despite my best attempts to send in help
He repelled all with great disdain

And then one day when hope was but gone
A mirror alerted me to change my thinking
I dug deep inside and recruited Will
My body would surely be shrinking

But Fat resisted and gave a fight
Giving not an inch until felled by a Diet
He couldn't get the hands to give in
And the taste buds to simply try it

So on this day with Fat but gone
I stay vigil as I guard my nether regions
For despite how much I would like to eat
I'd prefer not to give in to Fat and his corpulent legions

Mirror Mirror

Mirror mirror on my wall
Why or why are my legs so small?
Once a basketball player I would be
But gave that up when five foot three
Your eyes appear as mine always do
Bloodshot red surrounding a hue of blue
We share the same hair color and style
With a devilish grin and an evil smile
Oh sacred sage upon who I look
The answers I seek come not from a book
For what I ask comes from the heart
The answer coming before I start
So here I look as I always do
Every morning I share just with you
For as I shave and comb my hair
I place my future in your care
Though you just look into my eyes
You congratulate my success no matter the tries
Although your voice I do not hear
You are my only constant from year to year
While magic or wishes cannot be
I know you will always be there for me

A Friend

A friend arrived this very day
Someone whom I had all but forgotten
We'd lost contact for many a year
My memory returned while helping those down trodden

She was my anchor and my staff
Who helped me through all the bad
Yet when conditions changed for good
I left her without a word and feeling sad

For I had been like those I now help
Living daily with no hope or money
She had taken me in her arms
And assured me my future would be very sunny

For such assurance she did provide
Forgoing her very needs for my own
She became a pillar and a friend
Insuring that I did not face problems all alone

But when her words did come true
And my life became what I did plan
I quickly parted ways and left
Distancing myself from the old as I ran

Yet she found me in her travels
Seeking to assure me a friend she'd always be
For despite what I ever said or did
She'd always be there for me

A Smile

A dog
A donut
A nickel or two
When mixed
Together
They bring
Happiness
To a child
Of two
So remember
That things
Though simple
At first
When mixed
Together
Can make
You smile

A Child

I was just a child
A young boy of but five
Living happily on toys and Cherrios
How would I know
That monsters did exist
Outside my closet and bed
My innocence I cherished
Being the only thing I truly owned
But how could I protect myself
From those who were meant to help
When father or mother weren't home
It happened so quickly I never knew
My memory shattered with the pain
It took forty years to come back to me
The blackness releasing my heart in pain
Remembering things that should never be
Justice impossible for those long dead
The death of myself so long forgotten
Added simply as another scar on my knee
I cried a silent cry asking for God's help
To protect others from a monster's grasp
And to remind them in their nightmares
That we are just a child

The Eagle

A majestic eagle soared up high
So far above the sea
Surrounded by nature's clouds
A simple life so free

But looks can be deceiving
Especially when we don't know
All life has ups and downs
No matter where you may go

The eagle soars not for fun
His travels meant to feed
For his shadow signals death
Caution his prey must heed

Be content in what you are
Because life is what you make it
To some others you soar above
For living is as good as it can get

The Valley

The flowers blossomed upon the field
Such beauty wasted before men's eyes
Birds chirped happily in trees so green
Oblivious to the maelstrom brewing in the skies

Nature's music came to an abrupt halt
When the clanking of metal came near
The approaching voices of conquering men
Induced even the mighty bear to run in fear

No more beauty would the valley see
When explosions uprooted fauna and trees
What had once been a scene of immense beauty
Became splattered with man's wars and disease

Though nature's sculptors took a millennium or more
To grace mankind with both plant and animal
Man's armies need but a few moments to end it all
No unspoiled valley safe until man's wars do go

Darkened Wisdom

Darkened wisdom beset by dreams
Held hostage by thoughts of wealth
Logic misplaced by frivolous actions
Being true to no one but yourself

The gold coin misplaced by greed
Costs far more than it is worth
Precious gems and minerals remain hiding
Elusive wealth for those on earth

Value placed on things without virtue
The honor of one's word a silent lie
Roads taken without thought or remorse
Lend no substance to those that die

Take heed in who or what you are
Life passes quicker than the falling sun
Remember that some things aren't meant to be
Waste not your life before it has begun

A New Tomorrow

What we had once is gone
And tomorrow starts a new day
We failed to listen to reason
And just turned our backs away

The excitement we once felt
Grew old and died before its time
Were we just so young and foolish
To lose such happiness should be a crime

Your eyes did once fill my world
My life I would have gladly given
Today I only look into the void
Where are the feelings that were so driven?

Tonight we toast to auld lang sine
And cast away our sorrows
Although I will really miss you
For us there will be no tomorrows

Summertime

Hot summer breezes ruffle the air
Stillness becomes passion with only a stare
Long legged beauties all lined in a row
Young men with smirks just raring to go
The sun simmers both young and old
The allure of shyness gives way to bold
Summer vacation is such a sight
Especially to those with youthful delight
Who wouldn't give up the winter chill
Just to experience the summertime thrill?
So the next time you whistle that holiday fare
And huddle next to some fire out there
Remember the heat of the summertime sun
Vacations awaiting, it's time to have fun!

The Ceiling

The ceiling shattered without a sound
No applause arose as the glass did break
The years had taken a toll on so many
Never knowing the difference they did make

From Eden's tree to quest for power
The chains of restraint had been broken
No longer a stranger to change or sacrifice
Their existence no longer regarded as token

They'd given birth to thought and child
Their wisdom and wiles had seduced the others
Though deemed weaker their strength prevailed
They established themselves among their brothers

Times have changed as they surely do
Mankind no longer to be imprisoned by the ages
Women have finally secured their rightful place
Our future now to be written on their pages

Speak Not

Speak not what you do not know
Let your mouth not open too fast
For in this world there is much to learn
Take care not to let good ideas past

It's so easy to take a position
Without ever really knowing the facts
The need to support or to offend
Serves not to prevent verbal attacks

So place a smile upon your face
And bite your tongue when you should
For being right or just the best
Doesn't mean as much as you think it would

Lesson Learned

Do not fail me
Came the cry
As the harpoon
Hit the blubbery skin
The cable jerked
As the point
Entered deep
Causing pain within
The whale did cry
A wounded soul
As it plunged
Into the deep below
Cheers of joy
Turned to horror
As the ship's crew
Were tossed to and fro
An alarm rang
To cut the cable
But no man
Could act so fast
Man's greed
Sank quickly
A lessoned learned
But not the last

The Acrobat

Jump now ye acrobat
Fly up high tonight
Leap across the open air
Oh what a wonderful sight
Swing so freely high above
A net to catch a fall
Perform your magic just for us
Bring excitement to one and all

Your Grace

Although I walk alone
I feel your grace up high
I sense your presence upon my life
Your love embraces me from the sky

While I struggle to survive
Everyday filled with work and stress
I appreciate all you've provided
More fortunate than those with less

Despite the complaints you must hear
Especially when I'm down and blue
I'll never be able to make it by
If not for my faith in you

While I'll surely never know the answers
For being created and made as just me
Being allowed to be on this earth
No greater happiness can there be

Lies

The serpent slides so smoothly
From the soul to the mouth
Seeking to enhance its appearance
For those who cannot understand

Forked tongues appear to be evil
Until blanketed in rich fabrics and colors
Gullible eyes see nothing but acceptance
Nodding in appreciation of expectations

Scales assume the appearance of fine fur
Soft to the touch and pleasing to view
Despite protests from tactile sensors
The mind denies that betrayal could exist

A single serpent gives birth to others
A nesting of slithering creatures
That give life to unending aberrations
Beginnings and endings lost in the multitudes

The creator soon becomes the created
Losing the ability to distinguish its existence
Consumed in the entrails of reality
Unwillingly casting aside its own skin

Had one but learned from Adam
That deception begets unwanted children
Despite desires to be otherwise
A serpent will always be a serpent

Doubt

Agony beset by emotion
Struggles to attain freedom
From the chains of unrequited love
Cast aside for another

The heart that beat so fast once
Now hibernates in a cave of blackness
Void of happiness or salvation
Guarding the shattered gates of innocence

Dreams that once presented promises
Are left scattered across a field of lies
Bereft of the excitement from which they grew
Forgiveness drifting into the emptiness of life

Alas a tiny reminder of guilt
Remains burrowed insides life's temple
Gathering strength from all around
Soon to spread elation and happiness

Would things have been different
Had passion given way to logic
And God had intervened to deter
The very essence of his own creation

But who can now doubt
That the heavens have spawned goodness
From the entrails of what appeared evil
When a tiny heart begins to beat

Somehow

Somehow is but a word
When no effort is afforded

Why do you fail to take action
When you know what you must do

If you were but a house
Your windows would be boarded

To protect you from the unknown?
There is no phantom after you

I've known you the most
Throughout these long years

I confess you are a little strange
Especially when you make that smile

But you're the best friend I could have
Despite your faults and fears

For aside from your decision to delay
You'll always go the extra mile

Trying

Who can fault a person for trying
Failures are just a way of life
Perfection comes not from just knowing
It is the result of surviving through strife

Regardless of profession or hobby too
The search for excellence taunts us all
Attempting to do better ages with time
No matter how difficult to get up after each fall

The Creator has made us all in regal splendor
No matter how we think we've turned out
He's graced us all with his own perfection
It's for us to learn what life's all about

A Better Day

Does pretty mean anything if you have no sight?
What definition could it possibly mean?
If you cannot look to decide for yourself
How could you judge what you haven't seen?

If your ears never heard truly great music
Would you understand a much better sound?
Could you really discern what was really good
Or would you take the opinions of those you hang around?

We are such lucky creatures of nature
Most of us blessed with many senses for living
Yet we base our decisions on what others say
Preferring to read, watch, or listen for the opinions we're given

Take heed to live life just for yourself
For you have the ability to decide all alone
Don't let others control or rule your life
Your opinions never need to be cast in stone

So set aside your favorite magazine or TV show
And refuse to believe what they are trying to say
Look upon all you meet with a wide smile
For if you do you'll always have a much better day

Facade of Life

Darkness fell harder than normal
The collision heralding abandonment
Lost souls free to escape the shadows
Individuals of failed accomplishments
Lack luster testimony to life
Consolation received and returned
Troubled souls united as one
The heat of the evening
Serving to simmer sweltering passions
Yet to be discovered
But unleashed by the flicker of hope
Morning comes sooner than expected
Human cockroaches melt away
The facade of life returns

Wondering Why

Why do the stars always appear brighter
When life is just beginning
Why do days seem so much sunnier
When bottles are just for spinning

Why do appearances mean so little
When our eyes are bigger than our bellies
Why do croissants taste so good
When filled with jams and jellies

Why do answers always follow questions
When in truth we don't want to know
Why do we dream in color
When our lives are black and white like snow

Why do we do such things
When we know it isn't right
Why can't we appreciate ourselves
When happiness is within sight

Why do we forget about love
When things turn down with sorrow
Why do we always forget
When things always get better tomorrow

The Best

I stood on the precipice of time
My future to be decided by me
Though all alone I wasn't by myself
I was guided by a force I couldn't see

To go or to stay wasn't really a decision
My direction was engraved in fate
Though uncharted my path would be
It was created on my special birth date

Regardless of belief in destiny or free will
The trek through life is the same
We all need to survive to succeed
The results of which only we're to blame

Fear not what road you choose
For most roads are the same as the rest
Just strive to do with what you're given
And in your eyes always remain the best

Cleaning

Does it really matter that the house is a mess
The dishes are unwashed and the bed is undone
If no guests are due today who must we impress
I yearn to have things the way I wish
With no more clutter or things left astray
I see my house as if a bowl and I were but a fish
You relish the notion of drop and run
Where things are left when finished or not
And your attention is geared to fun
I try to be good and carry a blind eye
But when I need to jump hurdles inside
The lack of such cleanliness makes we want to cry
So I beseech you my companion and lover too
Please remember to pick up after yourself
Unless there is someone else you'd prefer to live with you

A Chosen Path

Sometimes I still wonder which road to take
Although my soles are worn and many are my years
I travel step-by-step knowing not my path
Only that it will be littered with hopes and fears

I see those who are much younger
Seemingly gliding effortlessly by
While I struggle with which direction to go
And still doubt my decisions or the reasons why

Behind me lay halls of gold and bastions of grief
Testimony to my journey as a man
Yet my best paths still lay before me
Beckoning me to decide as best I can

So I traveled as I knew I should
Sometimes taking an alternate route or two
Though some would have been much easier
Nothing would change if it meant losing you

Encounters

Sanctimonious responses to questions without answers
Fabricated remembrances of things never there
First time encounters both brief and too short
Ears that don't listen feigning to care
Eyes searching for truth but blinded by doubt
First impressions tainted by gross misconceptions
Hands clasped to signal a greeting
A wave of the arm and life goes on

Harvest

Light winds blowing
Fields of golden flux
God's finest eateries
Provided for me and you
Barley and wheat and corn
Waiting to be harvested
Nature's succulence slumbering
Twilight arrives
Another meal to be served

Eighteen

I once feared so much this very day
When all eyes turn to look at me
My life has passed so quickly
Wasn't it just yesterday I was three?

Sure I've experienced quite a lot
And seen much of the worldly sights
But as the days come and go
It is only now that I await the nights

Not because of what you may think
Or because I dread another year
It is because I am full of joy and wonder
And anxiously await as life's twilight draws near

The big Eighteen is just another day
For those of us of high spirit
We look into the mirror and see ourselves
And smile as we just grin and bear it

We are who we are, a happy sort
Who relish in all that life has given
For no matter how much we age going forward
We'll never just stop living

My Companion

When I gazed upon your eyes
I saw the hurt and sorrow
If I could buy you anything
I'd insure you had tomorrow

We spent a lifetime as friends
Racing both to and fro
From beaches, forests, and desert lands
There wasn't anywhere we wouldn't go

You've been my trusted companion
A savior for all these many years
You've seen me at my bad and best
And comforted me through my worst fears

There are those who'll never understand
The love that we both now share
But if they had experienced your spirit now
Who among them would not care

So my pet, my colleague, my cherished buddy
One last walk together we'll take
Know that I shall always love you
A better dog God could never make

Actions

Stop for a moment and look what you've done
Said the mother to the young child
The room was a mess with toys all about
Strewn haphazardly on the floor they were piled
Instructions were given to clean the room
A time limit was set for the feat
If corrective action wasn't done on time
There'd be hell to pay the next they'd meet
So the child was left to make amends
The chore much larger than he alone
Although he set about to prevent a spanking
His failure was already given and known
The mother took pride in ruling her house
She controlled her children with her hand
If they disobeyed and were bad
They had to deal with her reprimand
But no sooner had she left the little boy
She went to a cabinet and took some liquor
Drinking greedily she nearly drank a bottle
Not knowing that her son had seen her
And so it is that discipline is learned
For actions do speak louder than what we're taught
The little boy will grow up confused
For order lies in the methods we've sought

A Broken Heart

Blackness permeated her darkened soul
The only remnant of a lover's void
Eyes that did sparkle dulled by pain
Visions of happiness crushed asunder
A charming smile once carefree and trusting
Wounded severely by careless misgivings
Hope overcome by truth a partner to sorrow
Memories of better times bereft of emotion
A frail tear appears and fades
Another broken heart requires mending

The Astronaut

I worked for years to be an astronaut
It was my dream to fly into deep space
When I was chosen to join the program
My dream had come true to be given a place

But now I sit in my modular chair
My helmet fogging from some strange steam
Only moments before an alarm did go off
Telling me in seconds there would be an end to my dream

I think we hit an asteroid or two
For it ripped a hole in our craft's wing
I know we're on fire somewhere over there
The cause of our deaths it will bring

My companions and I had planned for this
Yet no training can prepare for your end
Although in moments we'll be memories
That we're not afraid we won't pretend

Despite it all we do remain calm
Our seconds are now but a few
Hopefully they'll learn from our little problem
And will make changes the next time they flew

With a final breath I now say goodbye
The intense pain I feel now already past
I take pride in being an astronaut
Knowing I'll be remembered by flags at half mast

Advice

Who can really counsel us
On what we do or say
Sages who don't live our lives
Or know how we spend our day

The Enron guys gave great advice
On how to make and spend
Graduate schools sang their praise
Until they realized it was just pretend

Presidents have gone to church
To advocate virtue and no sex
The Moral Majority voiced their support
Quieted when scandalized by an "ex"

Making money is all we're taught
From almost the day we're born
Although the Good Book is quoted lots
Its pages seem never worn

Alas this very day
I decided to seek advice
I ended up doing something I shouldn't have
And was arrested by the Vice

So this I say to all who care
Take counsel with some trepidation
For no matter what is said to you
Remember it is not their reputation

Passage of Life

Lightness of being bereft of sensation
A stark awareness of untied earthly bonds

A sense of completion unshackled from logic
A heart once filled with contentment and joy

Limbs dangle without purpose or position
Finality of inaction and incomplete errands

Eyes stare blinded not by light but by dark
Sight without seeing, beauty no longer to enjoy

Thoughts without purpose give way to the void
A mind submerged in sleep without end

Words left unsaid never to be repeated
The voice of silence sounds a deafening echo

Oratories given but never quite heard
Remembered by neither enemy nor friend

Time left unused is lost to us all
The passage of life never moves slow

Beauty

Long golden trusses
Touched by Athena's fingers
Her aroma fills the air
A fragrance that always lingers

Cheeks as soft as rose petals
Newly plucked from their stems
And prevails upon heaven and earth
Surrounded by only good omens

Lips as full as ripened plums
Desiring to be licked and enjoyed
She holds her heart in confidence
Emotions not to be toyed

The Letter

The letter fell off my lips
Accompanied by another few
They joined together in combination
Creating the first word that I knew

Da Da was what I said
My parents were quite amazed
As I added Ma Ma next
For my performance I was soon praised

The words continued coming
They spilled forth in great amount
As the months flew by and went
My parents quite soon lost count

What had caused so much joy
Soon became a major pain
For as the years did pass along
My parent's happiness turned to disdain

They couldn't stop my stream of words
Threatening discipline to stem the flow
No matter what the subject or matter
I was happy to let them know

Now that time has past and I'm a Dad
I cringe when I hear the baby chatter
For I know what will surely come in the future
But who cares, it really doesn't matter

God's Will

Achilles had a tainted heel
Samson wore his long hair
Goliath never knew to fear a stone
Alexander fell to failed health care

Strength at times is great to have
Yet we are all weak in many a way
Even the invincible have their fears
For in death we all do lay

Take pride in the talents you're given
No matter how trite or small they seem
For when used as they were meant to be
They can help bring life to a dream

Live each day with your inner strength
Believe in yourself and tackle each mountain as a hill
Do your best to be who you know you are
For your success is left to God's will

The Walk

I went for a walk
This morning
The sand
Comforted my feet

I enjoyed the sun
While walking
It's rays
Warmed my heart

I touched the water
Beneath the sun
It's coolness
Calmed my soul

I went for a walk
This morning
Nature's gift
For all mankind

Just Me

I felt the wind upon my face
Its touch reminded me of my wife
So light and yet so constant
The true love of my life

My years have been filled with wonder
Although times have been good and bad
While not as wealthy as others
For my special riches I am very glad

I've been blessed with more than gold
From children to material things
My memories are filled with hope and joy
And all the enchantment happiness brings

Like the wind my life flows by
Days ranging from gentle to angry
I thank God for my being alive
Living life as just me

Wait

I am afraid I must admit
Change is knocking at my door
What will come I do not know
Nor what plans others have in store

My direction had pointed north
But destiny altered my chosen road
Now I walk along a different path
Requiring me to have courage and act bold

A new job is always a daunting task
Tying loose ends before starting anew
Saying farewell to colleagues and friends
Remembering once there was a beginning here too

So now I go on my merry way
Challenges and tests await to greet me
No doubt I'll succeed as I always have
But I guess I'll have to wait and see

A Single Step

I took a simple single step
The first time in forever
I can't explain the elation I felt
For they said it might be never

That summer night is just a blur
The excitement racing in my veins
I'd had one too many beers I think
Before racing across those highway lanes

It happened so fast I couldn't react
My car no longer wanted to obey
I lost control when I hit one hundred
I remembered nothing else that day

The nurses told me I was almost gone
My life teetered between life and death
I've learned my lesson about driving drunk
And will remember this time to my dying breath

Wonderment

I gazed upon a single bird gliding amongst the clouds
With wings spread outward majestically; a king within his own
domain
I dreamed a moment in distant wonder and pondered about his life
To be so carefree and innocent; soaring so far above the nation
I realized then that we were much the same apart from feather and
flesh
We both soar above our concerns; life has been good and there is
nothing left to
attain
I know now that the lightness I feel has nothing to do with flying
My heart is full and overflowing; my mind gushes forth with
anticipation
I sensed your presence in my sleep but realized that I was wide awake
A vision of unfettered loveliness; Athena herself would grin with
pride
I closed my eyes to embrace the thoughts that satiate my very being
Contentment was just a vacant stare; having no substance until you
cast your smile
I thank the heavens everyday for giving me riches beyond silver or
gold
A chance encounter now charts my course; prudence dictates my
feelings I now do
hide
I would gladly cast aside all that is to journey forth and take flight
We are but two birds of a feather; enjoying the seeds of wonderment if
only for awhile

His Passing

Darkened clouds did set the mood
No sunlight needed for the occasion
A somber moment had now come
For we had lost a leader of our nation

The wind does whisper his words now
Saved within our souls and hearts
We pray not for his passing death
But to rejoice as each new life starts

For his wisdom and greatness saved us all
He lead us across our own Red Sea
Through his leadership we lived and prospered
To remain forever the land of the free

So as his body is laid to rest
Our final words said for his goodbye
We thank the Lord for giving him to us
For his passing we do grieve and cry

The Floor

Twenty feet pounded upon the floor
A ton of flesh moving forth and back
Buzzers rang and whistles blew
As the opposing teams readied their attack

Back and forth the players raced
A rubber ball the treasured prize
Up and down and into the air
The score of a point to make crowds rise

Arms and legs were in constant motion
A symphony of muscles to appease the eyes
Cheers and screams rang in the air
As the lead went to their chosen sides

Minutes passed as hope was shot
Careers rose and faded with attempts to score
The victor named at the final buzzer
Glorious excitement provided on the basketball floor

Since I Came

I walk in silence as a mortal man
Observing all life has to offer me
I came to see if salvation was possible
But that is clearly left to be

Since I came last nothing has changed
Although man has progressed in making things
Greed and killing are still prevalent
You still care not for what peace brings

I hold my tongue and say not a word
Long ago realizing fake prophets are all around
I pray to my father every night
To spare man from the thinking they're bound

I've been robbed and humbled by others
Again I live and walk among the poor
I tried once to recruit some followers
But man has grown more callous than my time before

You give great credence to religious leaders
Although they speak not for me or above
I'm filled with sorrow that you worship images
And seek salvation by kissing a hand in a glove

I hear the prayers spilling from your lips
Seeking my arrival and return
But I am here and you recognize me not
Overlooking the very thing you most yearn

This time around it's you who will die
For all men must pass away
Look into your hearts and see I am here
It is up to you to decide how you'll live each day

We Beseech You

God we beseech you to send another son
The years have passed without salvation
Your firstborn is said to have died for our sins
Yet peace exists today in not one nation

You have permitted us to hope and pray
Though we can't agree on whom we call
Sometimes we turn our cheeks and take the pain
But mostly we prefer to fight with one and all

We don't follow your commandments much
Although we act in your name all the same
When things don't go as we want them to
Because you didn't listen we rest our blame

We spend great wealth to get your attention
Our churches and temples are created for you
We worship for your love and forgiveness
And make sacrifices of the animals we slew

We've come a long way since the days of old
No longer do we crucify great men
Then again if someone said he was your son
No doubt we'd kill him just because we can

Star Struck

Star struck girls walking the streets
The smell of perfume and perspiration in the air
The search for stardom and elusive success
Lays waste to those who care

To be so famous with name in lights
Is a fantasy that few will ever see
Yet thousands flock to Hollywood's streets
To take that one chance just to be

Where is the allure that seduces the mind
Common sense dispensed and cast away
To journey forth and to take the risks
For the opportunity to be famous one day

While some may stay and others will go
Dreams fulfilled and others not to occur
Each day fills the streets with tearful eyes
Erasing lives as if they never where

Tears of Joy

Oh tiny little babies that kick inside of me
How anxious you seem to get on with your lives
If I could read your thoughts, I would surely know
That you anticipate your entrance into this exciting world
Already you know the pleasures of a gentle caress
And the closeness I feel sleeping in your father's arms
You've experienced the joys of sipping fine wines and champagnes
And tasting a simple burger and the sweetness of fresh fruits
By the kicks of your tiny feet, I know the excitement you know
When you hear the barks of dogs at play
Although you cannot yet see, I know that you yearn to look upon
The snow flakes as they drift just outside our windows
I can feel the rhythm move through your bodies as our stereo
Serenades you with a cornucopia of musical delights
I know you appreciate the sweet mutterings of two lovers and
All the tenderness that life has to offer when you feel my gaze upon
your dwelling
Despite all the trials and tribulations that you will one day encounter
You already know that I will always be there to watch over you
Most of all, you know the love I feel for you when my thoughts drift
to you
Tears well up in my eyes and slowly fall to my cheeks
Oh tiny little babies that kick inside me
Know that the tears you will soon shed will bring us nothing but joy

The Park

Amid the towering buildings
Rested a simple green park
Though small it had grass and trees
A place for children and dogs that bark

Though somewhat lost among the structures
It was home to birds and small creatures
Providing sanctuary to both young and old
A resting place for sometime teachers

Within its realms a new world did grow
A reminder that peace can exist amidst stress
Though street sounds could still be heard
It was a haven to relax and rest

Though man does continue to advance
At least they've remembered to keep some green
For this park represents the best of us
The part kept hidden and never seen

Fashion of Life

Slender legs guiding across the stage
Designer clothes draped across curves and chests
Flashing lights and music pounding in rhythmic beat
Today's latest exhibits of dresses, hats, and vests

The beautiful people all gathered in regal splendor
Amid gasps of excitement and cries of dismay
People's careers rising and falling on cuts of cloth
As so much colored raiment discarded as spoils of the day

But once the music stops and the lights glare no more
The masters of facades fade into their own creations
Only silicon, peroxide, tape, and replaceable hair remain
The reminders of hopes and dreams and surrealistic relations

But millions will beg and borrow and steal to be seen
In fashions created by those that they have no love for
To pretend to be someone else can create a special dream
For them there are only promises of life and the hope for something
more

The Fair

The ferris wheel twirled with excitement
Young children screamed their delight
Carnival music filled the air
The county fair was a wonderful sight

Barkers yelled about their games
Dimes turning into dollars for a bear
Exotic flowers and trees filled pavilions
Artists painted faces and dyed kids' hair

Horses and cows were paraded for prizes
Sheep and pigs to be showed and sold
Musicians played every type of music
Such fun for both young and old

Delicious snacks filled hungry stomachs
Little mouths colored by cotton candy
Young mothers stuck in continuous motion
Trying to clean messes with anything handy

But all things do come to an end
The last visitor leaves the exit way
Though the fair has ended it'll be back
What a wonderful way to spend a day

Summer Days

The waves crashed all around
Young surfers tossed to and fro
Life cleansed with churning breakers
Time passes never slow

Sun bathers strewn across the sand
Seeking beauty from high above
Surfboards floating in the ocean
Nature's calling for those in love

Pelicans skim the blue water
Seagulls gawk at the passerby
A myriad of smells great the nostrils
Marshmallow clouds frost the sky

Summer days gone so quickly
Vacation time passes like blowing sand
A day at the beach to be remembered
The thrill of living can be so grand

Without A Dream

Where does one go without a dream
With no desire to strive for things to be?
How does a boat steer without a rudder
When cast adrift far out at sea?

Do roads that have no purpose
Lead to destinations that don't exist?
Can a thought have any meaning
If its reason for being does not persist?

A mind can be a fertile vessel
If nurtured and grown with care
Why do we overlook those less fortunate
Pretending that they aren't there

We beat our chests to profess our glory
Sports and movies are regarded so high
We turn our backs on our children
Crime is rising yet we wonder why

So stop the trend that is now growing
Give pause to see what we've done
All children deserve to be just children
Experiencing life and all its fun

The Red Light

The signal turned red
But I didn't stop
I thought that I
Could really make it
Much too late
I realized my fate
My decision bad
No chance to brake it
The crash occurred
In my minds eye
For death comes
So very fast
To be an adult
I'll never know
This red light
Would be my last

Adrift

Cast adrift in a sea of dark alabaster clouds
The wind blowing aimlessly across a fertile mind
Dreams and thoughts of happiness once so possible
A life pirated by tainted treasure turned so unkind

One's vessel needed to carry hope across an ocean
Turbulent seas capsize only a ship filled with fools
Devotion and trust meant to protect us from humiliation
Life's journey altered by the uncharted course that we choose

No choice given to the creations we have been given
Passion's moments spawn legacies sometimes so cruel
The fate of young hearts soon lost to all forgiveness
Best intentions shipwrecked despite the goodness we do

No ark can save us from the thunder of own despair
Seas of discontent spill over and flood the field of dreams
The desire for good fortune drowned by the sadness
No salvation possible amongst such dire extremes

Remorse comforts not the grief in those once discarded
One's safe passage left floundering upon the empty shore
A future once bright capsized by misplaced adoration
A life left rudderless in unending misery forever more

Look Far

What is love without another
Can a mirror be so bad
An image cannot speak
Nor never make you sad

How can loving oneself be wrong
They say it is a terrible sin
If you can't love yourself
How can loving another begin

Who can fault adoring an image
One that lives but breathes not air
Is it narcissistic to love yourself
If you do it when no one is there

Self love isn't really terrible
When you consider what it does do
No disease or heartbreak will ever come
Nor child out of wedlock will ensue

So those of you who can find no pairing
Take pride in being who you are
Know that the mirror hides no secrets
To find love you needn't look far

Each Day

Though days do pass I remain as stone
So firm am I in my love and conviction
While the world may change and weather me
My heart is reborn by you with the coming sun

Such sadness and grief had I once experienced
Times of hardship and pain came and went as they do
When all seemed gone and hopeless and I felt so lost
An amazing gift was given and it happened to be you

Surely heaven had a grand plan when you did come
A chance encounter occasioned by the passing minutes
Yet my first glance told me He had sent me an angel
My life changed when we both knew we'd now be an us

Although we realize no pot of gold lies beneath the rainbow
And falling rain though romantic will still soak us to our skin
Knowing that our love thrives and grows ever so stronger
Makes each new coming day such a wonderful way to begin

Oh Mighty Ash

Oh mighty ash held in my hand
Gift me with your inner strength
Bless my soul with your aged wisdom
Help me succeed at any length

Let me see what others cannot
Make all men feel your might
May a thousand ears hear your thunder
Let them know you rule this night

I pray that you and I become as one
No greater foe will they ever see
Together we'll give meaning to your existence
No humanly power to prevent our victory

May grain and muscles merge together
Bonding man to nature as never before
Be straight and true in your resolution
Giving credence to what we have in store

So on this night let's work together
For two champions have come this day
Let them feel the sting of failure
With the first pitch made low and away

Tormented Souls

Tormented souls captured by greed
The search for riches always a dead end
Fortunes gained through deception and lies
Happiness gleaned from let's pretend

Gold and silver are cold to the touch
Only love can warm the heart
Friendships bought from shallow friends
Relationships ended before they start

Fancy cars and houses so large
Status symbols for those with many a secret
Years pass as do their morals
Simply road signs on promises not broken yet

Plastic cards in platinum and gold
Limits way beyond all possible need
To outdo others that are so similar
Teaching youngsters to follow their lead

Rich or poor are same as black and white
Each distinctively different than the other
No matter the platitudes or acceptance
Never a doubt each had a different mother

When life does pass we are all the same
No spirit can wear a fine ensemble
We each must know the value of our lives
For we take nothing where we will all go

Cry Not

Cry not for me children of God
Cry not for me this night
My Father's wrath is coming
Hold your loved ones tight

Years will pass as will your tears
For time has no meaning high above
The all knowing knows everything
Despite this He gives all His love

Though I'll pass as will you
Our life on earth but a blink
My departure at the hands of man
Gives pause to make Him think

Life will prevail as will your evil
The ability to choose given at birth
Salvation is yours if you but listen
Spend wisely your time on earth

Dreams

Though fairy tales exist not with our real world
Dreams can come true if prayers are merely spoken
The desire to be happy exists within us all
Our hearts so resilient despite the times they're broken

Though summer days now fade quickly away
The heat remains if we choose to take it for our own
What began as a simple smile takes life
Romance ignited by the seeds of hope we've sewn

While still so new a spark of hope now grows
Someday to be a conflagration if allowed to spread
Seek not to douse such flames with tears of doubt
Love so possible if words of commitment are said

So take my hand as we now walk into the future
Each day made brighter by the hope of things to be
Think only of the life now made possible by us together
Happiness so clearly visible for all the world to see

Heartbreak

Stifle not the tears of dreams gone by
Painful memories that breed within the soul
Awaken each day refreshed in believing in love
Romance waits patiently just beyond the things you know

Wear the face of happiness despite how life may turn so sad
For existence stretches not so far ahead
Within your grasp lies the world that you seek
Quiet not the words of possibilities that lie inside your head

Though love has been tainted it remains still pure
The search for the one thing true an arduous task
Our hearts yearn to trust the things we wish to believe
Disappointment carefully forgotten by questions we don't ask

Take comfort in the kisses that touch our lips
Better to have love and lost and to take a chance
Simple joys so possible amongst the joining of two souls
No hope will we ever have if we give up at first glance

Decisions

I remember so fondly the smell of fresh bread
The joy of running through the neighbor's sprinkler
I remember the smile across my mother's face
Oh the things we'd do just to insure we pleased her

So quickly the days passed as if in a blink
The days of childhood eclipsed by hormones that raged
We watched without notice as we became adults ourselves
The role of parent and child now reversed as we aged

Though filled with great love the grown child must make choices
The desire to please usurped by our own coming demise
With hearts turned heavy we decide our parent's fate
The passage of time so difficult to see through tear filled eyes

I now close my eyes and pray to Him who watches above
My own time approaching now close at hand
I pray my own children will become the adults they should be
The hardest decisions in life better left unplanned

Evil Twin

I can see not the frown on my face
Though I feel it pull at my skin
I'd gladly trade it for a small smile
But this day belongs to my evil twin

He comes and goes as he does please
His arrival occasioned by pangs of guilt
I fend off his coming as best I can
Giving way as my soul does fade and wilt

I seek salvation through holy water
Although He would never bless it as so
It clears the mind and eliminates confusion
Or so my evil twin would make it so

Though bonded together we are worlds apart
Despite the appearance we are the same
How does one ever regain happiness
When its loss is one's own blame

Darkness of Uncertainty

Awaken me not from the sleep of sorrow
My heart stricken by the loss of hope
Happiness once pure is now so tainted
A world without you I cannot now cope

Though wisdom is my trait I am lost
The songs of life but torture to my soul
Hands once clasped now wrung in frustration
A chance for resolution beyond what I know

Bravery exists not in a heart so torn
Passion cast aside by thoughts gone bad
Trust and faith tarnished by misspoken words
Purity of heart replaced by a face so sad

Yet miracles do occur or so I pray
A love once amazing still held tight
I pray He gifts you with clarity of vision
The darkness of uncertainty replaced by His light

May His angels guide you on your journey
The path between past and future your road alone
Yet I know together we can slay our demons
Happiness waits beyond what we've ever known

To Begin

Save me not from the life I live
Such joys surpassed by things soon vile
Happiness so brief quickly torn away
I pray the world to stop for just a while

My heart once pure did become quite dark
The underside of humanity seemingly enchanting
I turned away from comfort of my family
My journey to hell nothing I had foreseen

When gifted with love I turned my back
Moments of pleasure sought between the thighs
I lived for the moment no future had I
No chance had I despite the number of tries

Once gifted with knowledge I lost it all
My future squandered upon comments unkind
Life once sure disappeared before my eyes
The loss of my true love never again to find

With weary eyes I now lick my wounds
No words to express my failure yet again
For the chance to start this now anew
I pray for the opportunity to again begin

Remorse

Forget me not as my time is at hand
The coldness creeps slowly into my soul
My life is but over and now almost gone
To heaven or hell I know not where we go

With a heart once pure I now am dead
The passage of time simply a passing thought
Actions and events tainted by stolen pleasure
A passage into Heaven cannot be bought

Silken skin wrinkles no matter what we do
A moment of excitement forgotten in a blink
The desire for happiness buried in vile ecstasy
Our Maker sees everything no matter what we think

No lips will again caress my hopeful heart
The chance for redemption now only a prayer
I die alone my life not to be remembered
Love has no meaning when you're no longer there

No Dreams

No dreams remain for souls now lost
The river of pain flowing deep into their veins
Pleasure and suffering both twins to destruction
The search for satisfaction produces ill gotten gains

So warm the creature that resides inside
No room for love in a place so cold
Darkness takes hostage the prospect for love
Young lives wasted no chance to grow old

Desire exists but for passion it is not
Man-made elixirs more powerful than lust
Restraint not possible when hope is all gone
Misery consumes compassion in a life without trust

No modesty remains in bodies so spent
Their virtue simply currency to feed excess
Death waits patiently for what will soon come
Redemption not possible for those who can't confess

A Life Fulfilled

I lost a child although she didn't die
The sin of pleasure so sweet upon her breath
A life once full now has gone away
Dreams forgotten in the fog of coke and meth

So wonderful was she and I was so proud
My heart made whole by her special ways
Yet she changed and succumbed to the darkness
Artificial excitement creating not her happier days

Such pain have I that I always cry
A father's hopes for the best not to be
Words mean nothing when covered in fog
The way for salvation not for her to see

I feel as useless as a needle now spent
My elixir of life a poor second choice
A father's guidance overwritten by a mother's hatred
The desire to do what is right given no voice

Yet I'll pray to Him for her redemption
A chance for her to see a new and better way
Maybe someday my daughter will know His love
A life fulfilled from which she will not stray

Believing in Love

So beautiful the face of a person in love
Their eyes sparkle with such a special glow
Voices turned soft by things turned right
A special skip to their step wherever they go

Such a shame that such feelings don't last
The passage of time turning things old
Freshness tempered by familiarity turns stale
New found love doesn't remain despite what we're told

We believe in angels and things we can't see
Yet what we feel we allow to fade
Where is hope when we can't keep our futures
Divorced from happiness by laws man made

Revelation so simple if we but listen
The desire to stoke the fires we feel inside
We're blessed with such ability to remember
Still we forget feelings we shouldn't hide

Do what you can to never lose your passion
So much easier to refresh what you already know
Always remember that each day brings fresh newness
Believing in love will always make it so

Belief

I give praise my Lord for what I have
Each day a gift from your Kingdom
Though I once strayed and lost my way
My path was made clear by your eternal wisdom

You've bestowed on me such amazing talents
Few men have been given as much as I
Despite things gone bad you've watched over me
Still loving me although I've wondered why

You've shown me what forgiveness means
So blind was I to the cost of seeking pleasures
Your Scriptures have been given life by your hand
Your words not coins are truly mankind's treasures

I awaken each day but a humble servant
Giving thanks that each day begins anew
My life has changed since I regained my faith
Peace on earth so possible if others believed in you

Lessons in Love

When do we learn to fall in love
Is it upon the first drop of morning dew
Does God gift us with such amazing delight
Or do hormones alone search for a special you

So many hearts are left so torn and broken
Yet others filled with such wonderful grace
Does the need to procreate consume us all
Romantic feelings sometimes relegated to last place

When do we lose our senses and grow deaf
Failure to believe forgetting about trust
Reality lost in such fantasy and dreams
Separations so difficult although we must

Alone and together but never both
Eyes glazed over with sugar coated lies
Goodness and humility often just cast aside
Desire for lust and passion no need for family ties

No answer will be coming as we know it all
Falling in love the hardest thing we do
Only time and broken pieces guide us along
Lessons of love never taught in school

Mankind's Laws

No winter cold nor heat of summer
Could detain me from my duty
My soul was smitten by young love
Nothing could keep me from her beauty

Though far away it was but a thought
Time and space stop not one's desire
Mountains and lakes are easily overcome
When satisfaction is what we aspire

Thoughts of lust simply heat the loins
Blood races quickly when given reason
The heat beats loudly in one's ears
When nature announces the mating season

Take head those who are still young
Emotions care not for a good cause
For when an urge comes it takes control
Procreation doesn't stop for mankind's laws

Little Johnny Student

Little Johnny Student
Sat on his bed
His homework was unfinished
No wisdom filled his head

He spent yesterday playing
Video games were so fun
After milk and twenty cookies
His homework never begun

His parents didn't know
Or didn't seem to care
They were much too busy
Watching TV from their chair

So it is that Johnny lives
Falling further far behind
Another child's future lost
Society loses another young mind

A Special Angel

No words can express our deep felt sorrow
Our sympathy extended through the love we share
The journey of God's angels never comes when we expect it
Understanding such loss so difficult to bare

Take faith in trusting in His knowing wisdom
The path of our own lives never really known
He gifts us with such joy in having children
Their tasks sometimes completed before they're grown

Rejoice and take comfort in the birth of your babies
Though one now sleeps in His arms above
A special angel now watches over your family
An everlasting reminder of his Graces' love

My Plan

I see you there
In the chair ahead
It would be easy
To tap your head
The teacher looks
Right at me
She knows my smile
Something soon to be
I wait my time
For her to go
My plan is made
Preparing just so
With a quick grasp
I take your hair
To the ink well
It fits right there
I giggle with glee
The ruler does hit
It'll be two weeks
Before I can sit

In the End

So sad it is to see us pass
Our bodies lapsing into despair
Muscles once full of life atrophy
Our youthful selves wish we were not here

Brains once vibrant and so intelligent
Forgetful now that years have gone past
Memories of happiness become so dim
Lives so rich never meant to last

Stricken by age or nature's demise
Bright promises more gone than around
Time stops not for man or God
Passing minutes haste our passage to the ground

We're all destined to die upon our birth
The honor of living such a precious prize
Our ending is just a new beginning
Our futures different from where our body lies

The Light

A Christian died and was buried today
No longer a spouse to a Buddhist who cared
Upon his grave ashes were scattered
A Hindu's body forever to be bared

A Muslim prayed to the heavens above
Forgoing the hatred for his brother Jew
No violence existed momentarily in the world
Peace no longer limited to a few

The hand of God had struck from above
His patience giving way to despair
Disease and pestilence ravaged the world
Forever changing the desire to care

Religion defined not by who lived or died
The affect of death devoured as it pleased
Prayers and chants were but noises
His ears turned deaf by mankind's need

It was only when but a few remained
That religions realized they were the same
A lesson learned too late for us all
Man's failure to see that light was to blame

No Stop

No train stop will come this day
Hope gives way to what's in store
The passage of time just races by
The chance for redemption exists no more

A tattered soul beaten by life
Too many battles have left deep scars
Wounds never to heal with salvation
No answers to be found among the stars

Remaining breaths steal life from words
Final thoughts wasted upon forgotten fears
The need to love and to feel the same
A faded memory washed by falling tears

The chance to be all that really matters
A pillar to those young and full of life
Misplaced actions made for wrong reasons
Happiness cast aside by anger and strife

The dying mind thinks only of hope
The desire to turn back the shriveled past
A life wasted upon misbegotten pleasures
Forgotten forever with one's last dying breath

Grace

What is happiness when life is depressing
The ability to subsist limited to what we earn
Money slips between our fingers like liquid dust
Hope forgotten on luck that will never turn

God given talents lay hidden inside
Secured tightly away from those without cash
Brilliance restricted by unavailable opportunities
Potential discarded like unwanted trash

They say we are equal yet close their eyes
Salvation not visible for those who don't see
The cold touch of a needy stranger is chilling
Avoidance practiced to save one's own sanity

The desire to help is fueled by approval
Society pages adorned by those who don't care
Charity provided only if the cost is not personal
Those they pretend to help never invited there

Yet the human soul resolves to survive
Inequities forgotten when we sleep each passing day
For those downtrodden hope still does exist
His grace provided on our dying day

Games

The games that get played for the sake of joy
Distorted truths cast adrift in our lies
Innocent flirtations gain strength from liquor
The will to stop lost behind our wandering eyes

Too late the thought that asks to stop
No mercy given to those that feel no pain
A glance or a smile is all that is needed
To entice those weak of spirit to not refrain

A simple swallow can disrupt the future
Logic lost when thoughts fade in liquid dreams
Guidance given displaced by memoirs of pleasure
Misplaced trust is never as it seems

Yet time stops not the repetitive cycle
Faith in God eclipsed by belief in fate
Fallen souls never will become angels
The way to heaven stopped at St. Peter's gate

Forever Young

Although my age has been matured by time
My heart remains as young as I was new
Passion still remains unbridled within my soul
Romantic emotions reborn upon the day I met you

Giddiness and pleasure are not reserved for youth
Such feelings eclipse everything we truly know
Education teaches not what we learn about love
Lessons of life earned only from seeds we sow

Such thoughts have I that I did when once a lad
The twinkle in my eye matched only by my smile
When you're close by I can hardly ever breathe
My life sustained by your essence for such a while

I fear not writing the words given birth within my head
For silence has never caused a great love affair
May your eyes and ears be as though they are my own
Happiness and comfort taken from the things we share

So take my hand and walk with me into the future
Our path lit only by the flames that burn deep inside
May we drink from the fountain of youth between our kisses
Forever young together despite how our bodies age outside

Paths

I write these words in the heat of anger
Flames stoke the ambers of my disgust
Years have passed as once intended
Love cannot exist without first trust

You've speared my heart with vengeful actions
Memories once fond now turned so black
Where is the person who gave me meaning
Your dagger pierced deeply into my back

I gave my life and my soul to be only yours
Yet you squandered all that I once gave
You've accused me of changing so quickly
No further from the truth is the life I did save

I cast not a stone in your direction
Though boulders have rained upon my head
I grieve not for the future I had hoped for
No use have I now of our marriage bed

Be safe and happy as you move onward
Our hands no longer joined as one soul
May you find what you seek in the future
No happiness together on the paths we now go

Perhaps

No rest will I find as I do prepare
Exhaustion travels poorly on glistening skin
My thoughts are filled with ways to victory
Nothing else matters but the will to win

An athlete am I as I arise each morning
The need to excel exceeds the desire to survive
I regard my body as my private temple
Each heartbeat reminding me that I am alive

Though tempered by the restraints of time
I indulge in the thirst to be the one best
Leisure time passes with no need to ponder
Useless wastes of motion detract from my quest

Though young in age I am a devoted servant
I pray for His assistance to guide me along
Each day I learn and gain the strength of wisdom
I beckon my foes to hear my winning song

Success comes not to those who don't practice
For the investment in pain comes at a high cost
But such a price means nothing to all winners
Failure costs more if the spirit is forever lost

No doubt people can't see why I am so committed
They prefer to reflect on the short time that I play
They'll never know the exhilaration I get from winning
Perhaps they will understand on some future day

Smell of Cookies

The sweet smell of cookies awaken the past
Succulent delights from days so long ago
Thoughts of Santa and dreams yet to be
Preferring our fantasy than truths we shouldn't know
Brightly colored lights blinking on the tree
Reminders of friends and lovers no longer here
For a moment they're brilliant and all that we see
Faint memories of happiness we hold so near
Holiday carols elicit such joy and delight
Our days as children relived with a song
Things look differently when covered in snow
Feelings released after being hidden so long
We escape from our lives if for only a day
The spirit of the season warms all on earth
No matter our religion or what we believe
We all the more fortunate because of His birth

Instead

Sleep silently you of tiny hearts
Our Maker watches over you
Listen carefully for the whisper of His words
Dream of those persons who love you too
Take comfort in the blanket that keeps you warm
Seek peace in lullabies that soothe your soul
Fill your thoughts with smiles of those older
Pray for others like you you'll never know
So tiny you remain the hope of all man
Your future unwritten by hands so small
Great promise do you bear for those still coming
The key to salvation forever possible for us all
Enjoy your time now spent just growing
The thrill of existence lays outside your bed
Wish not for a time of being much older
For once here you'll wish to be you now instead

The Table

I look around the table and smile
For before me sits the lives I hold dear
Friends and colleagues and my relatives
Brought together from places both far and near

I raise my glass and toast you all
For without you my life matter not
Though we celebrate the passing of another year
It is I who am humbled by what you've taught

You've shown me how to laugh and care
Despite the things that make all cry
From you own frailty you've shown me true love
Forgiving my failings without ever asking why

While I've tried to be I was often bad
Your disappointment painted across your face
Yet you stuck by me and showed me compassion
Keeping room for me in your own special place

No fear have I had of the world out there
For I've learned that I can depend on you all
When things were the worse you were there always
If I needn't help all I had to do was call

While accepting the passing of time is quite hard
Much worse if on others one never ever depends
Life has no meaning if being alone is what we have
My greatest fortune is having such good friends

Popularity

From forlorn days to times of grief
I trudge through life without much flare
Invisible to most I exist without hope
If I disappeared no one would ever care

No home have I or place to stay
All I own cradled in a single suitcase
The smell of fresh soap is a thing I treasure
As are coins I gather from a stranger's grace

My dreams were much like those I watch
Forgotten laughter once filled that place inside
Yet life turned upside with the loss of my job
My dignity left as did my young bride

Though humbled by misery I retain my smile
Inside my head they still laugh at my occasional joke
Despite the smell of despair I do manage to subsist
Chances so few for those now lost and broke

So I plead to you with your civil wisdom
Are there causes greater than helping those like me
Why do you not see that we also need your help
Charity seems not possible for efforts without popularity

Seldom

I sailed across the sunburned sky
My dreams aloft in thoughts of grandeur
Stardust sprinkled down upon my brow
My time forever enraptured by heaven's allure

Rainbows took birth in droplets of pure honey
Problems forgotten within shades of grey
Clouds of promises yet to be alive
Memories without thoughts danced together in play

Hands clasped in unison for things yet to be
Forgiveness not possible without some pain
Souls bathed in love free to see the world
Infants given meaning in God's falling rain

Life is for the living so clearly now defined
Depression feeds only loneliness and the night
Spirits lifted higher by things now possible
Decisions made abruptly seldom ever right

Stardust

Stardust dreams amid fields of green
No laughter awaits those who cannot smile
Depression gives way to thoughts of suicide
Darkness overshadows life's failed trial

Hope once eternal crushed by those unkind
Marital vows forgotten with growing despair
Reconciliation buried beneath a soiled bed
Forgiveness not possible when souls don't care

Life gives birth to the death of all things
Romance no survivor among broken hearts
Hands once clasped together no longer touch
Unhappiness cares not where it ends or it starts

Holidays

No Christmas tree to decorate
Colored lights grace not my home
The smell of cooking arises not
Holidays mean nothing to those alone

Sing not your carols or similar fare
Angelic voices bedevil the lonely soul
Send not your cookies with little bows
No decision of which parties not to go

The laughter of children of so long ago
Gift wrapped packages in all their splendor
The clanking of glasses to celebrate the times
The remembrance of happiness all but a blur

The season brings chill and nothing more
My heart now frozen in such deep sorrow
The simple thought of getting invited to celebrate
Would make the holiday worth every tomorrow

For a Moment

Darkened skies spread across the plain
The threat of rain ingrained deeply in the clouds
Antelopes and buffalo race to overtake the wind
Beauty and pageantry never lost in heaven's bounds

Lightening gives birth to nature's electricity
Human and animal soul entwined in earthly delight
The scent of discovery arises from the trembling ground
Colors turn grey as light turns to night

The eagle soars amid God's regal splendor
Sounds of life serenade the majestic mountain peaks
A small brook nourishes life for but a moment
Gracing eternity for the serenity that mankind seeks

A single heart untamed beats in appreciation
God's glory praised by those without speaking
For a moment in time nothing ha been more beautiful
The purpose of life displayed before our King

From Heaven

Lost hearts and souls never to depart
The sky filled with anger and despair
Shattered dreams and hopes lost forever
Happiness vacant as though never there

Smiles once alive now buried inside
Crypts filled with love that could have been
No flowers grow in fields of weeds
Fertile minds laid waste by mortal sin

Hands once clasped now held in rage
Futures bright now buried in the dark
The winds of change stole all satisfaction
Reality remains in a world so bleak and stark

Love eternal extinguished by cruel perception
The search for truth forgotten by us all
How does one forget what truly matters
From heaven we too will all one day all fall

Happiness Again

Such darkened skies do come this way
The clouds of despair heavy on my brow
Thoughts of grandeur have all now gone
Love awaits not for me right now

With stricken heart I ply the night
No salvation granted those without a path
Tears of loneliness gather outside my reach
All hope crushed by my ex-lover's wrath

Roses once full have turned to dust
Sweet murmurings forgotten in a happier past
Hands once soft are now drenched in rage
Two lives strangled by love once meant to last

Yet I'll go on as I always will do
My head held high upon a pained dream
Once again I'll try to find the one
Finding happiness more difficult than it would seem

So High Above

Oh rain filled skies that cry so high above
What pain do you carry that we cannot see
Has our lives disappointed the heavens so
Are the best things in life still yet to be

Though full of promise if we could but keep one
Best intentions cast adrift in hopeless despair
Shards of truth lined in fantasies so real
Ambitions crushed by those who do not care

We hear His displeasure in the echo of thunder
Yet on deaf ears do we not listen
Though learned we heed not His ancient counsel
So tarnished are our souls they'll never glisten

While guilty not for actions of those now dead
The seed of our ancestors still affects us today
Dust covers not the misdeeds of mortal man
Salvation not possible for those who've lost their way

Slumbering Giants

I call on thee oh slumbering giants
Awaken from the sleep of things unreal
Arise from your graves of forgotten stories
Return to the world of warmth you once did feel

Man's progression has set aside his need for a hero
Though belief in demons and saints is now accepted
Gods do not exist except on comic pages
No more are your names heard in prayers once said

Technology and religions more powerful now rule our thoughts
Aged wisdom lost forever to printed words and books
The need to be different left to clothes and tattoos
The desire to believe in a difference brings dirty looks

Progress has forced us to accept what we are taught
The need to dream is slowly fading with each day
So important is it now for man to see the unexpected
Please help deliver us before we surely lose our way

Dating

Such energy we spend upon finding a mate
We primp and we prepare yet we have our doubt
First impressions give way to the inevitable choice
Decisions become such a chore on who to take out

Who or what we want tempered by what we see
The magazine and friend cloud the need to think
The ideal mate seems to be what others want
Disappointments can lead the best of us to drink

Gallons of coffee and wine drown the desire to speak
Words given birth once grow old when repeated again
Stories about one once so bright soon pale
Such are the ways of single women and men

Reality

The water cascaded upon silken thoughts
Dreams drowned in the ecstasy of being alive
The future now bathed in things yet to be
No rain of doubt falls upon those safe inside

What had been lost was cast adrift in sorrow
Unhappy memories set upon Viking ships aflame
Flowers of hope placed lovingly in streams of tears
The flood of emotion overcomes those who share blame

Sipping from the well of life no longer a chore
The thirst for truth slides so easily past the tongue
Tomorrow brings the desire to soak in one's life
Reality dampens not the spirit of those who think young

Such Truths

Hark ye angels that seek my sleep
My eyes grow heavy with despair
A heart once so full of happiness
Has given way to the grief out there

Romance did blossom so deep inside
Entangled limbs happy upon silken sheets
A simple smile brought forth encouragement
Love now cast forth upon the streets

Strength of two was a formidable foe
The outside world could not break inside
Unhappiness gave birth to such misery
Cherish forever lost to the groom and bride

Words once spoken have faded in the wind
Ears turned deaf by thoughts so unkind
The unseen ending came at such a price
The search for such truths both will never find

Without

Somehow lost but never found
A soul eclipsed by motion
Things remain still for never more
The heart now bereft of emotion

A cancer traded if only we could
Death by disease a chosen route
A lost romance kills from within
The hopeless situation removes all doubt

The tender touch now burns so deep
Dreams left scattered upon diamond cliffs
Shards of memories stab deep inside
A once happy future replaced by what ifs

Lovers once no longer keep the facade
The thread of truth entangled by a lie
Reconciliation buried beneath evil thoughts
Without any happiness all romance will die

Electricity

Don't you know what life is worth
Days wasted before that digital screen
Fingers dancing to and fro in great haste
Understanding not what purpose it does mean

Vocal chords succumb to a life soon decayed
Language given new meaning by new found text
Eyes grow and shrink with colors flashed too quickly
Dreams forgotten and replaced by what appears next

Technology overcomes the need to be a human
Metal and plastic creating a convenient identity
With the flick of a switch and a simple click
A curtain of insecurities hides what you want to be

Yet is there no desire to wish Edison never lived
Electricity possibly left to sail away with Ben's kite
Progress moves quickly when we forget to live
Love awaits only those who venture into the night

The Sun

The rain fell lightly to cleanse my soul
Redemption granted as I lay dying
My life was squandered on a deserted wasteland
Grief stricken faces washed by eyes now crying

So young am I that I cannot remember
No happiness will I gain from a family
Loves and heartaches are things I'd cherish
Nothing now possible in a life not to be

I fear not the impending darkness
For even the young can accept their demise
What I fear is the gifts I might have carried
Giving no longer possible with the past sunrise

A bright light waits not for those in battle
It is nothing more than the flash of a firing gun
The last sight I'll see is the reality of wasted existence
My life to pass with the coming of the sun

For My Companion

As surely as you read these words
Know that my presence is still at hand
Though I've left the body of who I was
When you sleep it is next to you I stand

While my wit and humor are whispers in the wind
My words now echo throughout the heavens
While you cannot hear what I now say
My love grows outside the world it transcends

Jake and I are once again together
Our days now spent in heavenly play
We spend our time enjoying what we share
Such great excitement greets us now each day

You needn't hurry to come and join us
As man and dog are doing as we care
We'll bide our waiting watching over you
Making sure your safe and sound down there

So dry your tears and toast us both
We've now in a place without earthly sorrow
Take solace that we'll wait and love you forevermore
Our paths will cross again on some future tomorrow

Chess Pieces

Grey haired gentlemen sitting
Chess pieces in slow motion
Lives once filled with excitement
Now boring and bereft of emotion

Hopes and dreams once so alive
Tempered by the passing of ages
Success once so very important
Testimony left on dog eared pages

Sagging skin so tight when so young
A remnant of what life used to be
Eyesight failing without much notice
Vision no longer needed to see

Yet smiles appear on forlorn faces
Victory still possible to those now old
Life changes only the position of the pawn
Each passing minute more valuable than gold

No Stone

I felt the tear so deep inside
No cure possible for the unseen ailment
A broken heart mends not alone
Love lost from words once never meant

How fast the flame fades from the bright
Wide eyes once beaming now just glare
The thrill of newness tarnished by age
Togetherness replaced by what we cannot bare

Hands once clutched hold empty dreams
Promises of happiness no longer spoken
Sheets lay unruffled by passionate touches
Romance forgotten by two souls broken

No smashed bone or laceration hurts as much
The need to be loved such a desperate thing
One desires to sleep throughout the day
Hoping happiness tomorrow will surely bring

Jake

They say a picture is worth a thousand words
Expression not as equal upon printed paper
Yet to touch and see is truly so much better
A memory of presence something we prefer

They say only a child can bring us happiness
No pet can match the intended inner feelings
Yet such orators never knew you as we did
A companion who taught us what a family means

They say a dog is really only but a dog
Devotion created by the things they are fed
Yet they didn't see the love you gave
Each day ending with joy as you raced up into bed

They say that we all must pass in time
God's gift of birth given with eternal living
Yet they never knew you loved to race ahead
Our own futures secure in a path now left unseen

They say a picture is worth a thousand words
Our memories refreshed by a taken photo
Yet we'll smile when we walk by your picture
Our family reunited on some future tomorrow

Alone

Flowers adrift on a sea of blue
Floating remnants of beauty once alive
Colorful funeral pyres fading from vision
The current removes any chance to decide

Memorials mean nothing after years elapse
Reminders of thoughts no longer there
The departure of the soul loses all meaning
No one remembers when no one is there

From birth to death our lives are swept away
Our courses set by events not our own
No matter how much we love or loved
At the end we all die alone

Our Family

So quickly the years have passed for our family
Each Christmas a new promise for better things
We've survived through the bad and enjoyed the good
Our best times together despite what reality brings

So proud am I of what He has given to our family
Brothers and sisters and a mother to admire
Fortune has surely blessed me with such amazing treasure
With the love of my family there is nothing else I need or desire

Men may come and they may one day eventually go
Yet no love is stronger than that shared between us
For when the day comes to a close we have each other
So reassuring it is to have relationships built upon trust

Now as we celebrate this holiday time together once again
Know that I will keep my love for you close to my soul
Though time and distance may now and soon separate us
Realize that I'll be thinking of you wherever you may go

While others may never understand what we do share
Take pride in being a part of our little special family
For when you need us we'll always be there together
Five very amazing women for the entire world to see

Wail Ye Women

Wail ye women cry your fears
Let your voices rise into the air
Cry and scream to awaken the masses
Let the world know of your despair

Pray to the heavens for man's transgressions
Shake unknown souls until they can hear
Remain silent no longer to satisfy others
May their knees tremble when they see you near

May your sons and daughters no longer suffer
Young lives squandered upon a foolish cause
Seek to establish their right to exist
No more sacrifices to fulfill man made laws

Take back your silence and assail the guilty
Men of politics and riches never shed blood
Have them volunteer the virtue of their own children
Let them recover their bodies from worthless mud

Stand together united with hands clutched tight
Know your bond is mightier than a sword
A single voice joined by others can take a nation
The prospect of your success something they cannot afford

The Loss

I sit alone as is always the case
The thought of friends a passing thought
So enamored have I been with my work
Only now realizing what money has not bought

Each passing day I grin and smile
Loneliness kept hidden so deep inside
Yet late at night when my drunk is gone
I resign myself for failing to have tried

Though while at work I am everyone's buddy
All who surround me adore and worship me
Yet when the day is done they never say goodbye
No desire to stay unless the drinks are free

I dread every passing holiday
So fearful am I that no invites will come my way
Yet I clean and decorate my lovely home
Yearning that just one guest will make my day

I take full blame for everything that has passed
My dance card was once so overflowing
I gave up all I was for those I loved
The loss of one's life never to be foreseen

Two Souls Bonded

Walk not alone into the void of life
Other hands were made to take you there
Where two feet there should be four
Loneliness exists not if unto yourself you care

When the fear of desperation clasps your soul
Let yourself feel the warmth of His touch
Your existence was made not to be forgotten
Though at times we all fail to remember as much

From the first sounds that escape at our birth
We seem destined to forget why we cried
Close your eyes and recall why you are here
The purpose of existence belongs not hidden inside

So take my hand in yours as we walk into tomorrow
No light needed to guide us on our way
Together we'll journey along an uncharted path
Two souls joined for eternity as we discover each day

Youth

Youth is so intoxicating
Stimulation gained by sight
Memories lost by fascination
The search for skin so tight
Liquor can't begin to compare
Satisfaction gained by impure thought
Possession is merely fleeting
Reversal of time can't be bought
Elixirs give pause for a moment
The quickening of life hidden by cream
Facades of rejuvenation swallowed freely
Realities of success merely a dream
We all once had what we now want
Yet so eager before to see it pass away
Maturity reminds us what we now treasure
A lesson remembered until our dying day

Life Is Too Short

No darkness do I find in the light
Sunshine desires not to hide the soul
Clouds swim lazily across heaven's pond
A heart warmed by affection makes love grow

Close not your eyes to the things you see
Even those blind know the sound of despair
Enjoy the beauty of this magnificent spring day
Greedily steal the moments for when you're not there

Life is too short to spend within the shadows
The coming of night speeds only your coming demise
Let the light of the sun give you pleasure
Happiness awaits with each coming sunrise

Coping

Something snapped within my mind
My vision faded from color to gray
Thoughts once clear become quite jumbled
No more happy memories would come today

Evil thoughts filled me with such anger
Previous failures resolved to become alive
Things once simple became misplaced misery
Tendencies once kept hidden exploded from deep inside

Neither good nor bad had any meaning
A black darkness eclipsed the essence of my soul
My fingers clenched into fists so vengeful
The contortion in my face demanding others to go

Had a weapon been ready for my solemn taking
Surely Satan would have urged me to attack
For those around I cared not for anyone
For ungodly deeds there would be no turning back

Yet the moment passed as it did arrive
A strange peace quietly covered me with hope
A hand touched my heart and reassured me
A faith in God the Almighty helps us all cope

The Dragon's Breath

While the dragon's breath did burn our skin
Its tempered flame did not char our soul
Though then but a child our memories are still fresh
Nightmares elude us not despite the things we know

The pain runs deep and chills the tortured heart
Love hurts when stolen by those who take our youth
Wounds appear not upon the flesh of those so young
The dragon's wings cover not the forgotten truth

Ears once deaf now burn with new found reason
The voices of children heard not except in nursery rhyme
Our protectors saw not the results of youthful despair
The loss of innocence regarded not as though a crime

They turned a blind eye to what was a family secret
Yet years hide not the ruins of things we did dread
No words or actions can ever return our lost trust
Love grows not where dragons once lived and tread

No Fantasy

No winter winds do now blow
The coming of spring close at hand
Fragrant flowers expel their aroma
Happiness gives birth across the land

Young hearts soon become all a flutter
Thoughts filled with feelings set free
Birds give praise to Heaven's abundance
Coming sunsets so quickly become posterity

The reason for existence no longer daunting
Even a young child can see the unseen
A simple thought explains earth's treasures
Our own failure to understand what it does mean

For once a year our burdens are forgotten
Our soul refreshed by the chance for recovery
Give praise to Him who gave us our breathing
Enjoyment of life needs no pretend fantasy

Descent

Decades fly past as the body ages
No phoenix to rise from the ashes of youth
Flowers blossom not in fields of maturity
The desire to grow old so far from the truth

Lines soon etched on faces once flawless
Brilliant glowing eyes no longer do shine
Movement once joyful gives way to inaction
The desire to move quickly disappears with time

Soft strands of hair become coarse to the touch
Shimmering colors fade as does out thought
Memories take precedence over new experiences
The secret of youth can never be bought

Cosmetic clowns mock our appointed destiny
Plastic facades shield not the dying cell
The internal clock stops not through deception
Modern technology never preventing man's decent to hell

Magic

So soft the notes that bathe my ears
Such tender music soaks my living soul
To listen awakens the reason I'm alive
My very being much more than I know

My heart explodes with such amazing delight
No need to read to understand unspoken words
Likes leaves of the fall the sounds fall in order
My thoughts take flight as though a flock of birds

Such enchantment do I have as if in a spell
Mankind's magic gifted through a musical thing
With a breath or a touch I can almost disappear
No humanely body needed for feelings they bring

Yet so strange that we seem to forget what we hear
For music is God's earthly present to all mankind
Purity of being given by Him for His children to enjoy
Purpose given to the love we hope someday to find

About The Author

Robert Steiner is a former Air Force officer, Fortune 500 executive, business consultant, inventor, and entrepreneur. He is also a novelist and a children's book writer. He holds a Bachelor of Arts in Economics from the University of California at Santa Barbara and a Master's in Business Administration from Pepperdine University.

He lives in San Diego, California.

Proof

Made in the USA
Charleston, SC
28 August 2010